If your style is streamlined and modern, celebrate. A contemporary interior is perfect for kids: bold color and sleek surfaces make a marvelous backdrop for toys, paintings, and accessories. The rules are simple: things must be practical as well as looking good, and children must respect what the whole family shares. Don't think that little ones are naturally inclined to dayglo colors and cute motifs. Credit them with good taste, involve your kids in planning their spaces, and give everyone license for fun and a free rein.

children's spaces
from zero to ten

children's spaces
from zero to ten

Judith Wilson

photography by Debi Treloar

RYLAND
PETERS
& SMALL

For this edition.
Designer **Pamela Daniels**
Senior editor **Annabel Morgan**
Location research **Kate Brunt**
Production **Susannah Straughan**
Art director **Gabriella Le Grazie**
Publishing director **Alison Starling**

Stylist **Judith Wilson**

First published in the United States in 2001
This compact edition published in 2005
by Ryland Peters & Small, Inc.,
519 Broadway
5th Floor
New York
NY 10012
www.rylandpeters.com

10 9 8 7 6 5 4 3 2 1
Text © Judith Wilson 2001, 2005
Design and photographs © Ryland Peters &
Small 2001, 2005

ISBN 1 84172 871 3

Printed and bound in China.

contents

introduction

Kids get everywhere, whatever space they're given. Newly arrived, the tiniest baby has enough equipment to kit out a world traveler. And, when your child becomes mobile, not a square inch of your home will remain sacred. Children are noisy, exuberant, and come with stuff by the crateload. They may drive the style queens among us to the very edge; yet without them, home would be too pristine a place.

This book won't maintain your hard-won, carefully designed space at the expense of your kids' physical and creative freedom. It won't

teach you to stencil a teddybear border, either. Instead, there is plenty of inspiration here from real families, with real kids, who prove that children and great design can co-exist happily, without either party having to compromise on style. Armed with practical surfaces and effective storage systems, parents can reclaim communal living areas within a matter of seconds at bedtime and enjoy being grown-ups again. And your kids will appreciate a vibrant, stimulating environment that is practical and relaxed, too.

Whether you're adapting a sophisticated, child-free zone for the arrival of a new baby, or starting from scratch because your small children have just outgrown a current home, some serious thinking is required. Plan all the practical aspects first, and the design and decoration will be a breeze. Your kids' needs may seem obvious, but their demands change with alarming speed. This is even more crucial with a new baby. Impossible as it may seem, that chubby infant kicking on a blanket will soon demand a space and life of its own.

A baby's first room needs tranquility and comfort, for infant and parents alike. Keep things simple with clear colors, quick-access storage, and a great view from the crib. Sensory touches add magic; perhaps a wind chime or tiny twinkling lights.

rooms for babies

1

THIS PAGE AND OPPOSITE: In a baby girl's nursery, a whitewashed antique crib sets the tone for a simple yet pretty room. Pastel-painted pegs hung with tiny dresses brighten white walls (below left). Painted pieces of board with old-fashioned wooden clothes-pegs attached allow for an ever-changing display of pictures, family snapshots, and paintings—there's always something stimulating for baby to contemplate. Open shelves (bottom left) are a user-friendly way to stack baby clothes, but allocate one alcove to each clothes type to avoid muddles.

A baby needs little in the early days, though department stores might try to persuade you otherwise. Many infants don't even move into their own room until three months or beyond, perfectly content to swing in a cradle at their parents' bedside. Nevertheless, a new arrival does need its own room, for changing diapers, storing clothes, and to house a nascent collection of toys. A small room is fine. It is cozy, and most toddlers would rather play in the family space downstairs than in a bedroom.

The main nursery basic is a crib. Simple styles are both practical and chic. More enticing options than traditional varnished pine are beech or cherrywood versions (though they will cost more), white-painted wood, colorful melamine, or decorative ironwork. An antique or retro-style bed can look beautiful in a pared-down room, but for peace of mind, check that its dimensions meet current guidelines and always buy a new mattress. A bed with slatted sides that are removed as the baby grows up is a sensible, cost-effective option. Pick the plainest style you can find.

Frilly, character-emblazoned bumpers will spoil the look of a simple, contemporary nursery. A padded bumper is a good idea because it protects restless little heads, but choose one in solid colors and with quilting, not ruffles. Cotton sheets and blankets are the other basics. When your baby is a year old, you can add a baby pillow and quilt. Nursery manufacturers have become increasingly inventive in recent

years, so blankets and sheets now come in every shade from pretty pastels to vibrant hues. It's fun to pick and choose between different coordinated ranges, or add a retro piece or two. Team a pink gingham sheet with a tangerine blanket, or add a home-made appliqué pillowcase to perk up plain white linens. A large single motif on a blanket looks more stylish than a tiny repeated design.

The diaper-changing area should be efficient and fuss-free. Resist the temptation to buy a special unit; it will soon be outgrown. A chest of drawers at the correct height, with a plastic padded mat on top, can double as a changing area. Store all the essentials—diapers, wipes, and creams—in the drawers immediately below, hidden away from inquisitive toddler siblings. Alternatively, place them on a sturdy shelf hung above the chest but still within arm's reach. If you have enough space, consider designing a custom-made unit. You will need alcoves for clothes, cotton balls, diapers, and so on, with a discreet pull-out or pull-down changing surface. If the changing mat is going to be on permanent view, pick one of the trendier designs. Funky fake grass or cloud images have a distinct edge over teddy bears. Hang a mobile above the mat: kids' mail-order catalogs often feature abstract ones, like trendy clips from which you can hang your own choice of postcards or photographs.

A low, comfortable armchair is a must for feeding. Get a slipcover made in a sturdy, washable fabric—bright denim, robust linen, or terrycloth. If there's enough floor space, beanbags in jelly-bean colors or wipe-clean vinyl cubes are great for babies learning to sit up or crawl.

Keep the room looking modern with fuss-free window treatments. If you'd prefer little ones not to wake at dawn, use blackout lining. A window shade, Roman shade, or wooden shutters are simple and neat; or, if you'd

THIS PAGE AND OPPOSITE: This double divan with surround on a tubular frame is ideal for a toddler who has outgrown a crib, but is not yet ready for a junior bed. In this room, strong color creates a bold contemporary mood—the egg-yolk yellow walls, purple drawer unit, scarlet quilt, and lime chair are stimulating and jolly. The practical clothes storage includes a rack for dresses and shoes (opposite below), while a chest of drawers doubles as a changing area.

THIS PAGE AND OPPOSITE:
With its sloping ceilings, an attic room makes for a bright, cozy nursery. Take advantage of a skylight view by placing the crib directly under the window, but don't forget a blackout blind or shutters to cut out glare. Toddler Scarlet's room proves that pink and white, that classic little girl's color combination, can be fresh and pretty instead of fussy and twee. White walls, a white crib, and a neutral carpet provide the basic backdrop, while clear, cool pink accessories provide decorative accents.

rather have curtains, bright or strong pastel solids, checks, or children's motif fabrics make the best choices. If you choose the latter, go for classic children's characters; they look more stylish than today's garish and over-publicized images. Or look to the more exclusive fabric houses, which often carry whimsical, abstract kids' designs at reasonable prices.

Plain painted walls and an easy-care floor create the most restful environment for a baby. Choose colors that you like for the early years—babies don't form their tastes this young. Whitewashed walls and a neutral floor are a perfect background for colorful accessories. But if you (and baby) need stimulation, paint one wall in a bold shade like cherry red or turquoise. If you prefer soothing pastels, stronger tones like lavender or duck-egg blue make the best background for primary-colored toys. Try painting abstract shapes: stripes or giant dots look good. Don't forget the ceiling—babies spend hours on their backs.

Crouch down by the crib and experience your baby's-eye view, then give him or her intriguing moving stimuli. Can your baby see through the window and spy trees, or view clouds through a skylight? If not, reposition the crib. String the ceiling with colorful Chinese lanterns, party bunting, or paper mobiles. You don't have to cover the walls with pictures, but you and the baby need something to look at. Initiate a personal collection now: a framed baby handprint or informal black-and-white baby portraits are more arresting images than most conventional children's art.

Use imaginative lighting to add a creative dimension. If there's an overhead light, install a dimmer switch, essential for checking on the baby at night. Plunder both adult and children's lighting departments for unusual options. There are "magic lantern" children's lamps, which splash the walls with gentle color and movement, or consider a lava lamp, strings of tiny flower lights, illuminated globes, or punched-metal lampshades that cast pretty patterns. Buy a pack of light-up stars for walls and ceiling, to glow long after the lights go out.

THIS PAGE AND OPPOSITE:
The simple, neutral look
won't suit every parent or
every baby. One way to
customize a tiny room—
often the only space
available for a new baby—
is to douse it in color. In
baby Archie's bedroom, the
walls are transformed with
zany stripes, while the crib
was chosen for its innovative
silhouette and zesty lime
color. For similar stripes,
paint walls a strong base
colour—hot pink was used
here—then use masking
tape to mark stripes of
varying widths. For simpler
splashes of color, paint
blank artists' canvases in
bold shades and hang them
around the room.

OPPOSITE AND BELOW, LEFT AND RIGHT: **Not all babies have the luxury of their own room. Sliding doors partition off this crib from an open-plan loft (below left). A crib in a corner of the parents' room can be individualized in small decorative ways, with baby photos (below right) or lengths of colorful bunting (opposite).**
BELOW CENTER: **Give plenty of thought to storage; then get a carpenter to build it to your specifications. This cupboard has a pull-out changing surface and tailor-made box to hold wipes, plus shelves for diapers. It also acts as a divider between the baby's sleeping space and play area.**

You'll probably need more space for baby clothes than you expect. Little shirts and sleepsuits make quite a pile; then there are gifts of clothes waiting to be worn, as well as outgrown garments. A closet isn't essential. Instead, choose a generous chest with plenty of drawers, which can be updated with a coat of paint or contemporary handles. A giant laundry basket is a must for a fast turnover of clothes. Wicker baskets, zinc tubs, or colorful plastic crates stacked on shelves or tucked underneath the crib will all make clearing up easy.

Your baby's room needs to be no-nonsense, but it must be safe and cozy, too. Anticipate the investigative crawling phase by keeping curtain pulls short, trailing cords clipped, and socket covers on, with a high shelf for any out-of-bounds items, and bars or catches on the windows. If you have a wooden floor, add a rug for softness, or choose a good-quality, plain wool carpet that cleans up well. Sisal and coir are a little too rough for soft knees. Just as you would with any room in the house, strive for the perfect ambience. Everyone should feel tranquil and calm in the nursery. You'll reap the reward of planning for simplicity: neither you nor your new baby knows quite yet what their favorite things will be.

Little girls adore pink, but they love baby blue, dreamy lilac, and grass green, too. Give your daughter a clear, pretty canvas onto which she can stamp her personality with favorite things, and organize it sensibly, so it's easy for her to clear up.

rooms for girls

2

THIS PAGE AND OPPOSITE: Converted from a hall in the basement of a Victorian house, Cordelia's bedroom is a triumph of clever space planning. The bed is scaled down to fit the room's narrow proportions, yet still holds toy drawers beneath and a large bookshelf at its foot. Behind the headboard wall is a full-height closet. If a room needs more light and planning regulations permit, a new window adds novelty. At night, this one is shuttered with wooden discs. An all-white room needs a splash of bold color for fun. Choose a small area and work through the color wheel as years go by.

66 *I like the windows in my bedroom. They look like balloons!* 99

CORDELIA, AGE 4

Most little girls love pretty things. But give your daughter a break from the classic, flowery bedroom and instead provide her with a fresh, contemporary take on the look. Crisp fondant colors or an all-white room provide the perfect background for little girls to display their special treasures. For tomboys, more muted shades and quirky, abstract patterns are appealing. Guard against reliving your own childhood fantasies on your daughter's territory. Just because you were denied shocking pink as a child doesn't mean she'll want it now.

If you're unsure where to pitch the style of the room, look to your daughter for inspiration. Amazingly, even a three-year-old will have strong opinions, so talk to your little girl about her favourite colors. If she's still too small, observe the things she's naturally attracted to. Does she reach for pink frilly dresses or a brightly colored T-shirt? What colors does she choose when painting? These little clues can provide you with an excellent decorative starting point. Keep the details flexible so you can change things around as the years go by. Painted walls rather than wallpaper, display space for treasured accessories, and classic furniture all make for a relaxed, easy bedroom. Stick to simple styles and a streamlined layout, and the room will look effortlessly fresh and modern.

When a toddler turns two and graduates from a crib to a bed, it provides a timely moment for reassessing the bedroom and making stylistic changes. Focus first on the hard-working furniture, planning colors later. Basic pieces won't differ hugely from the baby years, but now a good bed becomes the central focus. Invest in the best mattress you can afford. Children may be light, but they need firm support, and a good-quality mattress should last for ten years. Think long and hard about the style of bed you choose. Girls will go through myriad fads, from Barbie-doll fever at five to seriously sophisticated at ten. Work backward. If a classic style with a contemporary twist seems suitable for a preteen, it can be made appropriately childlike for the earlier years.

Select a distinctive frame to make the bed a strong focal point and save studio beds for teenagers or spare bedrooms. Plain and simple reconditioned hospital beds look cozy for tiny children, especially when accessorized with a graphic animal-motif duvet or piled high with candy-colored floral pillows for older girls. Self-assembly sleigh beds are another versatile option. The high curved sides mean little ones can't fall out of bed, and the ready-to-paint frame can be reinvented in bubblegum pink, then powder blue, followed by hot orange as girly crazes wax and wane. If you only need a headboard, be inventive and customize one. In place of a traditional Goldilocks-style curved headboard, choose a more contemporary rectangular shape, with cutout circles or hearts. Think fairyland, think woodland grotto, and create a headboard from picket fencing or gold-painted wood adorned with giant faux gemstones.

Canopied and four-poster beds, bunk beds, or sleeping platforms prove irresistible to girls, as well as providing extra space for sleepover friends. For adults squeezed halfway up a tiny ladder

THIS PAGE AND OPPOSITE: With its patterned pillows, white walls, and shutters, this five-year-old's bedroom strikes the right balance: it's pretty, yet not inappropriately boudoirish. Children adore whimsical touches, so scour thrift stores for unusual buys. Here, the lighting includes teacup sconces (above left), an illuminated goose, and a tiny dressmaker's dummy, while the bedside radio is a car (above right). Ready-to-paint composite-board furniture (left) can be customized with simple motifs like dots and hearts. If a little girl has a large room, a double bed can offer a comforting oasis.

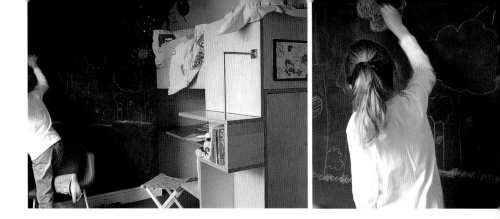

trying to make the bed, they may be marginally less popular. Yet you can have great fun designing a special bed. A simple wood or tubular metal four-poster affords plenty of decorative potential and looks very contemporary. Frames can be draped with brightly colored net one year, homemade strings of shells the next, or with inexpensive, glittery sari silks for older girls. Or you could create a canopy with a plain mosquito net handsewn with fake flowers. A raised bed can usefully accommodate storage or a desk beneath, and for stylistic continuity can be custommade in materials used elsewhere in the house. Practical plywood, painted composite, or galvanized steel are all options, and will be softened with colorful bed linen and teddies.

If you have decided on the bed, let your daughter make some choices, too. Gradually amass a varied selection of bed linen so as she gets older, bedmaking becomes creative rather than a chore. Snap up odd sheets or pillowcases in department-store sales or hunt flowery retro eiderdowns in thrift stores or yard sales. In the same way that little girls love to pick and choose their dolls' clothes, they'll relish the chance to mix and match pretty pillowcases and quilts. Provided they are from a complementary

THIS PAGE AND OPPOSITE: With its funky materials— rubber floor, plywood bed, and polypropylene chair— eight-year-old Lucy's bedroom also has the basics for a teenager's den. A series of plain, colorful surfaces creates a versatile canvas that can be dressed up with floral beanbags or kept simple for a tomboy. An entire wall covered in blackboard provides endless entertainment. A custom-made platform bed in painted composite board or plywood, as here, is not only a brilliant space-saver, but also creates a cozy, self-contained unit for a child.

❝ *I love my bed, because it's nice and cosy. I keep lots of my special things up here.* ❞

LUCY, AGE 8

palette, crisp checks, solids, and florals mixed with white will look wonderful jumbled together on the bed. Extras like an embroidered baby pillowcase, cozy travel blanket, or appliquéd top sheet make the final effect more individual. For a particularly modern bed, choose solid linens in a number of hot shades—perhaps a cerise pillowcase and quilt cover teamed with a lime bottom sheet. All white is no fun for a color-conscious child, but if you're insistent, at least customize a white quilt with satin appliqué or a button trim.

The bed may be top priority, but storage comes a close second. Plan for, or with, your daughter by writing an exhaustive list of everything she needs to keep in her bedroom, from toys and clothes to decorative inessentials. You will need flexible storage to accommodate a child's eclectic collection of possessions, which can range from masses of tiny toys to bigger items like a doll house. Not everything has to be put away at all times, but each item should have a home. It's simply not true that children are naturally messy. Most love to be neat. It's up to you to provide sensible storage so clearing up is quick and easy.

Provided the room is large enough, the chicest and simplest storage option is to put in a closet with floor-to-ceiling, flush-fitting doors all along one wall. Behind this clean façade you can provide a multitude of different-sized shelves, roomy enough to hold individual crates for small items, yet deep enough for piles of sweaters and jeans, and including space for a clothes rod. Open shelves may seem a tempting option for finding toys at a glance, but closed doors are preferable. At bedtime you want the room to be peaceful, without a child's favorite toys temptingly on view. Once the doors are shut, it doesn't matter how messy things are inside. The doors can be as simple or as inspired as you like.

THIS PAGE AND OPPOSITE:
Girlish schemes need not be
flowery: pale sugared-almond
tones look equally feminine.
In this seven-year-old's attic
eyrie, eau-de-Nil walls, pastel
bedding and butterflies do
the trick. For a little girl who
values privacy, create a hideaway. String suspension wire
between walls to divide off
the bed area, and add a voile
curtain. "Found" objects lend
romance: here, a cabinet is
home to an eclectic mix.

THIS PAGE AND OPPOSITE:
Many little girls love a heady mix of florals, and three-year-old Cyprus is no exception. Avoid over-co-ordinating floral patterns and add splashes of a primary color, perhaps a scarlet pillowcase, to give essential bite to the sweeter pastels. Mixed with an iron bedstead and painted wooden furniture in strong shades, the look is fresh and modern rather than traditionally rustic. To focus attention on a floral bed, play down the rest of the decor, sticking to white walls and plain curtains, and add scatter cushions for a grown-up feel.

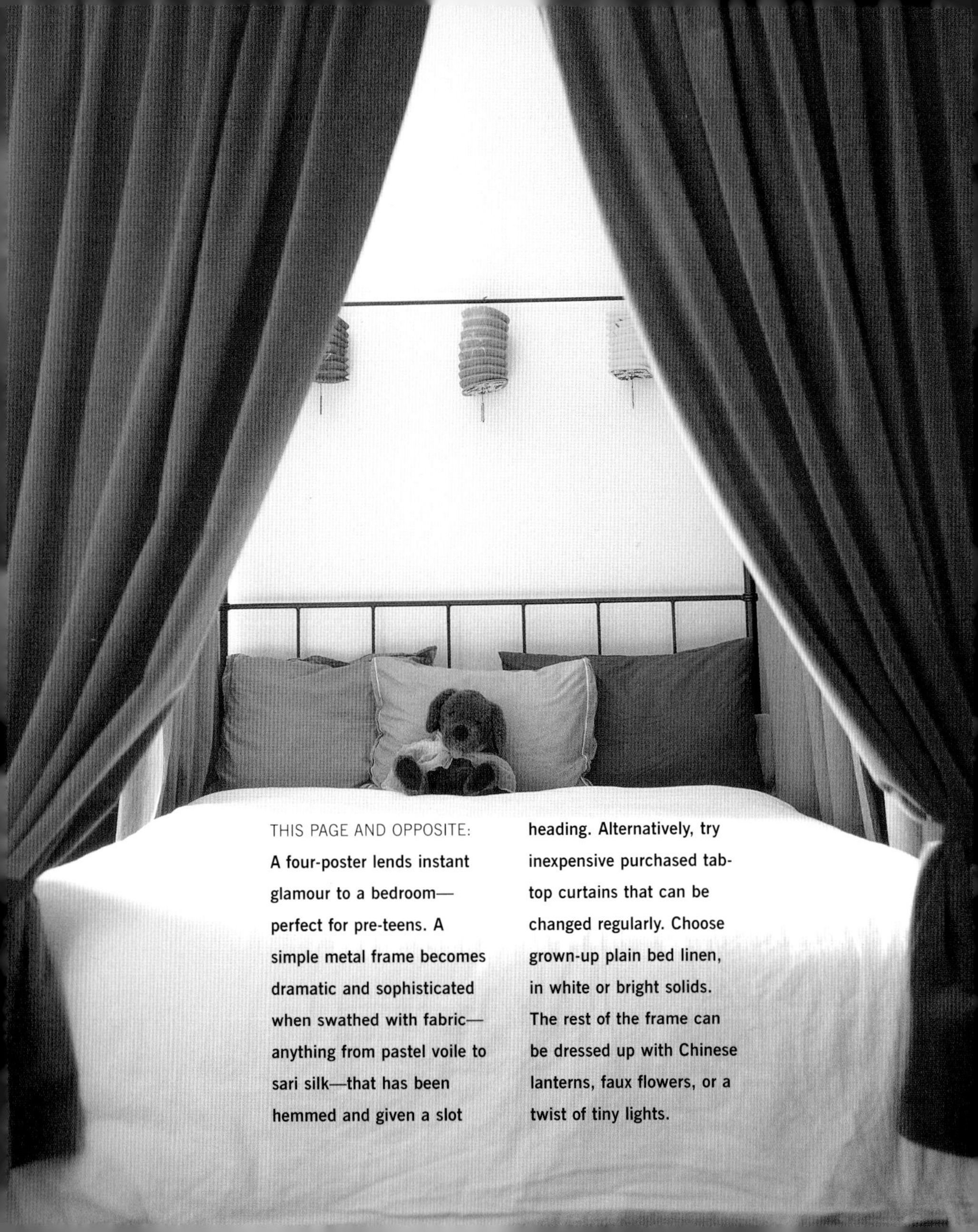

THIS PAGE AND OPPOSITE:
A four-poster lends instant
glamour to a bedroom—
perfect for pre-teens. A
simple metal frame becomes
dramatic and sophisticated
when swathed with fabric—
anything from pastel voile to
sari silk—that has been
hemmed and given a slot
heading. Alternatively, try
inexpensive purchased tab-
top curtains that can be
changed regularly. Choose
grown-up plain bed linen,
in white or bright solids.
The rest of the frame can
be dressed up with Chinese
lanterns, faux flowers, or a
twist of tiny lights.

In the same way that little girls love to pick and choose their dolls' clothes, they'll relish the chance to mix and match pretty pillowcases and quilt covers.

Paint them the same color as the wall and add small handles positioned at child height, and they'll all but disappear. An eggshell finish provides an ideal surface to display artwork. Alternatively, you could make doors from clear plastic, aluminum, or plywood for a contemporary spin. If you are saddled with a chest of drawers that's practical but unattractive, site it in an alcove and put on modern, flush doors.

Ideally, you should provide an area for your little girl to draw and do her homework. Purchased dressing tables and desks are often frustratingly small and have complicated detailing. Take a tip from contemporary interiors and provide her with a long, low worktop with wall-mounted shelves above. It could be painted board or covered in stainless steel or colorful laminate. Site the computer here; underneath put crates on castors for toys or books, a second stool for a friend, even a cabinet with lots of shallow drawers for coloring pens and paper. If you add a mirror, a counter can also double as a dressing table and display space. It's important for display areas to be comfortably within a little one's reach, not high up on a shelf. Don't be controlling about what she wants to show off. You may not appreciate a collection of glittery nail polish and papier mâché fruit, but beauty is in the eye of the beholder. She, in turn, will appreciate an arrangement of grown-up fresh flowers. Little bowls and baskets will keep hairclips, jewelry, and nail-stickers in order.

Most children relish a colorful environment and will want to be involved in choosing their favorite shades. Painted walls are much more flexible than childish patterned wallpaper and provide a cleaner background for the inevitable jumble of toys. See what happens when you offer some paint color charts to your little one. You may be amazed at her innate good taste and the shades she picks.

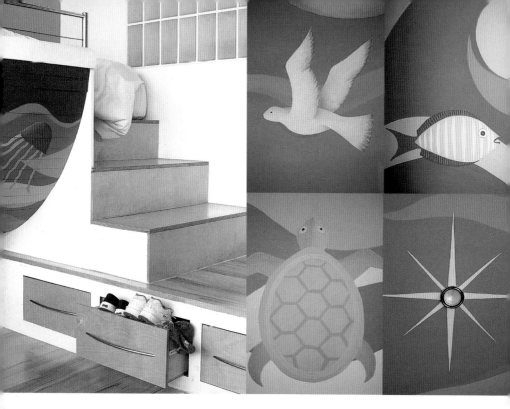

THIS PAGE AND OPPOSITE: Both sexes will relish a theme bedroom, and don't assume girls will want a fairy's grotto. This little girl's boat bed, with its seafaring theme, has delighted her since her toddler years. Provided the painting is professionally done, a full-scale mural is the perfect antidote to a nondescript bedroom. Keep the images bold, and consider incorporating a shaped bed. This bed is imaginative, beautiful, and practical: it was custom-made for the space, including storage drawers below the steps.

Older girls will enjoy dipping into sample pots of several different colors and painting large squares of cardboard to prop up against the walls while deciding on a shade. Follow the same color rules as you would anywhere else in the house. Jolly brights like sherbet yellow or cornflower blue are stimulating, but it's best to restrict them to a single wall so the effect isn't overpowering. If your daughter is dead set on pastels and you're not, shift the tone a little to an off-pastel for a more sophisticated effect. Or suggest some positive alternatives: substitute lilac for pink, or soft leafy green for the more usual pale yellow.

If you're set on a contemporary style, and your daughter wants an ultra-feminine retreat, it's still possible to tread a stylistic fine line between the two. An exuberant flowery fabric will please you both, provided it is tailored into a Roman shade instead of full curtains, and teamed with a simple aluminum bed frame and plain sheets. Alternatively, keep walls and windows simple, with white paint and white self-patterned voile, but choose floral bed linen. Butterfly or leaf motifs are good alternatives to flowers, or you can achieve a girlish look by customizing a white shade with sequins and covering floor cushions in shell or eau-de-nil satin. If you can't agree, and want to avoid making expensive mistakes, fit the window with a plain roll-up shade, simple metal pole, and curtain clips. Style-conscious little girls can change the curtain with anything from a length of Liberty lawn to dotted Swiss. Cover the nursery armchair in cheap, washable white cotton duck and make pillows together. Citrus-colored linens with a bright monogram, or pink denim with purple cross-stitch, will look trendy and smart.

Every little girl needs a space to display her artwork, photographs, or poems on the wall. Conventional cork or padded pinboards are often too small. Much more stylish is a large piece of steel, powder-coated in a shade to match the walls. Use magnets to attach drawings, pictures, and cards, allowing displays to be changed frequently without stripping the paint from the walls. Glass clip-frames or painted wood frames arranged symmetrically are a chic way to display favorite photos or to create an informal family tree. Don't overlook the decorative potential of childish paintings. Imaginatively framed school artwork, with a bright mat, can turn a naïve illustration into stunning Pop Art.

Remember that good as you want your daughter's room to look, it is her own private haven, a place for chats with friends, somewhere quiet to do homework, a retreat for dreaming and scheming. Providing privacy for children is vital. Help your daughter to delineate her territory from other siblings so she can be alone when she chooses. You could mark her door with a giant gilded initial, or get a metalwork company to cut out her name in stainless-steel letters. Alternatively, she might enjoy hand-painting her monogram using special calligraphy. Agree on a more imaginative sign than a hand-scrawled "Keep Out". A necklace strung with colorful lettered beads and hung over the door handle is far prettier. Use ingenuity to provide her with a cubbyhole for secret things. If remodeling is on the agenda, could a small alcove be inset into the wall? Perhaps a tiny built-in cupboard could be set into a boarded-up fireplace.

Bedrooms should be fun, so indulge in a smattering of kitsch. Search for funky extras: a beaded curtain, a glitterball to spin from the ceiling, a leopard-print cushion. Most mothers are still little girls at heart. If you like something, chances are your daughter will, too.

rooms for # boys

For boys, create a cool den that's fuss-free and has versatile furniture for imaginative play. Raid the color spectrum for inspiration—scarlet, leaf green, indigo— then team with robust surfaces like rubber and wood, so no one worries about the inevitable scrapes and dents.

3

Boys care passionately about their bedrooms. From around five years old, most know instinctively what accessories and motifs are "cool" and will want to incorporate at least some into their private space. They may fuss less than girls about an overall scheme, but are obsessive when it comes to the smaller details. What boys need most is empty floor space—as much as you can spare—and plenty of storage so their myriad collections, from toy soldiers to racing cars, can stay sorted and ready for play. Furniture that offers a bit of action—ladders to climb, platforms to scoot along—goes down a treat, too.

It may sound sexist, but rule number one is that everything in a boy's room should be robust. When play gets rowdy, he won't think twice about bashing the headboard: plan for that from the toddler years, and everyone can relax. Therefore a wall-mounted, enamel-shaded bedside lamp is a more sensible option than a fragile Japanese paper one, and a sturdy metal camp locker more practical than a canvas armoire. Imagine each piece of furniture being jumped off, climbed on, or moved around as part of a pirate-ship game or impromptu kickabout, and you'll get a realistic picture.

Little boys need efficient, well-planned storage to help keep their things in order. For toys, the ideal storage system combines plenty of small drawers, crates, or boxes for compartmentalizing tiny toys, with bookshelves and perhaps taller storage space for larger items.

LEFT: **If space is tight, then choose a single, all-purpose piece of furniture, with drawers for clothes, shelves for books, and a spacious top that can double as a display area for treasured possessions. Coats and shirts are easily hung on wall hooks. The bedroom is the ideal place to display a child's artwork, so fill one wall with a giant pinboard.**

" I like my room because it's clean and tidy."

FLINN, AGE $2\frac{1}{2}$

With this in mind, it makes sense to pick scratch-resistant modern materials like laminate and plywood, or painted furniture that can be easily touched up with a lick of paint.

In a boy's room, too, the bed will be the central focus. Why not take that literally, and situate it in the middle of the room: a bunk bed is much easier to turn into an imaginary ship or climbing frame if it's easy to get at.

In terms of changing tastes and needs, boys have a steeper developmental curve than girls. They still need a cozy sleeping nook at the age of three, but by five are ready for a more adventurous, classically boyish option. There are alternatives for tackling such shifting criteria. Either buy a generous-sized junior bed for the baby stage, and get a serious boy's bed once your son outgrows his crib. Or invest in a grown-up bed at the age of two, and make it inviting with a jolly quilt and accessories for the early years. A bunk bed is an excellent option. Your son can sleep on the safe lower level until about the age of six, and graduate to the higher level when he feels ready.

Boys, as much as girls, appreciate having a fuss made over their bed. It does not simply represent somewhere to sleep, but is a child's special safe zone as well as being a potential platform for imaginative games. Ready-to-buy options might include dark wood or painted *bateau lit* and sleigh-bed frames, simple iron bedsteads, colorful melamine platform beds with storage drawers, or sturdy tubular metal and canvas camp-cot styles. You'll get the best fun and most individual results by dreaming up a customized bed. In an attic, a built-in bed can be slotted in beneath sloping eaves, with roomy pull-out drawers beneath, all paneled in tongue-and-groove. For an older boy, a simple plywood platform becomes something special and looks modern supported on giant castors or sophisticated tubular metal legs. Alternatively, you could commission a carpenter to build a boat or a spaceship pod around a standard studio bed. A theme bed can look stunning, provided the rest of the decoration in the room is simple and clean-lined.

OPPOSITE: **A treasured collection of colorful vintage children's reading books bring a splash of color to Flinn's snug bedroom.**
BELOW: **A child-size washbasin is a boon in the bedroom—great for encouraging teeth-brushing. Crosshead faucets are easiest for little fingers to turn. This is also an ideal spot to site a medicine chest to hold child-related basics, but hang it high on the wall and make sure it is securely lockable.**

THIS PAGE: **Instead of
sludgy shades, choose
quirky, vibrant colors for a
trendy, bright boy's room like
eight-year-old Gabriel's.
Floorboards can be coated
with tough, glossy floor
paint for a practical finish.
In a small room, a bunk bed
(even if the child doesn't
share) is a great idea, acting**
as a chill-out area and
climbing frame as well as a
sleepover space for friends. A
custom-made desk is more
fun than a traditional design.
Wall-mount as much
furniture as possible, leaving
space for all the essentials
of the boy zone—a soccer
table, punchbag, dartboard,
or basketball hoop.

❝ I like my bed, because I can sleep on the top bunk. Sometimes a friend stays over and sleeps underneath. The colors are great because they really make my room stand out. ❞

GABRIEL, AGE 8

For most boys past the age of five, a bunk bed or raised sleeping platform is a dream option. These days many stores stock tubular metal bunk beds, which are more stylish than the wooden variety. If you'd prefer to build a platform bed, modern materials like stainless steel, plywood, or painted board are all good options. Think about safety and access. There should be a guard rail along the open side of the bed; one that a little body can't wriggle through in the middle of a dream. To climb up, a ladder is the most conventional choice, but make sure it's anchored securely in place. Metal rungs firmly attached to the wall beside the bed also look good. If there's room, a staircase created from giant building blocks is an imaginative way up to bed. Boys appreciate little extras, including mini-slides, rope ladders, or clip-on ramps (perfect to join two bunk beds if boys are sharing). Tie-on canvas or sailcloth panels are also good for imaginative play.

A raised bed frees up more floor space for play, so is a boon in a small room. Storage cabinets, a generous run of worktop or, with a lower bed, lots of pull-out drawers, can be variously incorporated underneath. Whatever bed you choose, when you plan the remaining bedroom furniture, try to find slim, streamlined pieces that don't encroach on valuable floor space, or movable items that can be pushed up against the wall during energetic games. Make furniture on castors a theme—everything from a chest of drawers to a low play table. Even better, clear the floor with wall-mounted shelves for books, baskets for miscellaneous bits and pieces, hooks for clothes, and even ceiling-suspended seating—perhaps a hammock or a swinging pod chair.

BELOW: **An antique dark wood bed will grow up with its owner. Here, the look is prevented from becoming too adult by a quirky mix of accessories: a giraffe-print side table, flag-emblazoned wall, and checked and patchwork bedding.**

Little boys need efficient, well planned storage to help keep their things in order. Most boys have minimal interest in clothes and in putting them away, so devise a simple storage system. Open shelves in a closet are the easiest option, but label each section clearly for T-shirts, jeans, and so on. Alternatively, build a series of box-shaped cabinets at child height all around the room, with each one devoted to a certain category of clothing, and fitted with a different-colored wood or stainless-steel door to resemble a school locker. The top of the cabinets can be used for sports trophies or toy display. A clothes rod isn't a priority. Instead, give your son a long row of child-height hooks where he can hang up his pajamas or anything else that has been strewn across the floor. Don't expect him to line up his boots and shoes neatly. Instead, provide one big basket, and agree that this is the designated place for all shoes at clear-up time.

The older a child gets, the more time he'll spend playing in his room. For toys, the ideal storage system combines plenty of small

crates or boxes for compartmentalizing little things (cars, Lego, plastic animals), bookshelves, and perhaps taller storage spaces for larger items like a pop-up tent or sports equipment. Settling down to play is much less enticing if toys are in a muddle, and most children are intensely appreciative of a freshly straightened bedroom. A simple wood or melamine unit, with alcoves for slotting in toy crates, is a very sensible option, and looks cool and modern when the crates are painted in a rainbow of funky colors. If you have the budget, look in contemporary furniture stores for dayglo polypropylene pieces—drawer units on castors, for example, or folding tables—all of which provide trendy, versatile storage that will grow with your child. If space is in short supply, giant shallow boxes on wheels can be built to slide under the bed, though they should have plenty of dividers.

Indulge your little boy's passion for complex structures, be it Lego or an elaborate cowboy fort or toy castle, and make sure that you give him a proper surface for displaying them.

BELOW: **Some boys like their bedrooms to be uncluttered and no-nonsense. Brighten the army camp look with a few outrageous touches. The giant Stars and Stripes and faux ponyskin pillow make this room as cool as a teenager's den.**

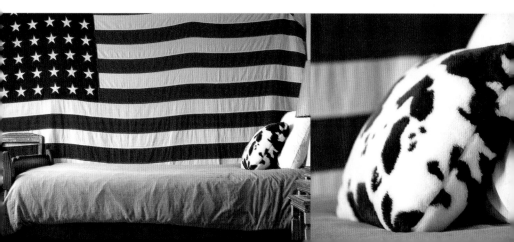

THIS PAGE AND OPPOSITE: Brilliant saturated color on every surface, from walls to furniture, turns an ordinary bedroom into an entertaining playroom, usually the best option if a boy has a large, sunny room. Don't stop with the walls: paint baseboards, closet doors, the bed and bookcase, all in vivid candy shades. Dark floorboards will balance the vivid color, while a cotton rug makes for comfortable floor play. In this five-year-old's room, the startling walls are matched by equally vibrant bed linen—a riot of crazy stripes, animals, and exotic fruits.

Give your little boy a display area that can be devoted to treasures like special gifts, homemade models, and toy cars. A thick shelf mounted above the bed and painted a bold color is a great choice.

The floor is not the best place because special treasures will have to be removed for cleaning. Instead, provide a low table and instruct everyone that this is no-go territory. Cover the tabletop in something indestructible, like stainless steel or oilcloth, so it doesn't matter if there are glue spills or paint splodges while craftmaking is in progress. In addition, little boys need a desk or computer table for working at, complete with task lighting and a good chair: there are plenty of groovy swivel seats available. Also give him a display area that can be devoted to treasures like special gifts, homemade models, and toy cars. A thick shelf above the bed, perhaps painted a bold color, or a stainless-steel catering shelf rack for older boys, make great choices.

Little boys play constantly on the floor, so flooring should be hard-wearing and attractive as well as providing a smooth surface. There's nothing more frustrating than trying to race cars along badly sanded wooden boards, or to arrange army platoons on bumpy sisal matting. Far more practical, and infinitely more stylish, are painted or waxed wooden boards, wood laminate flooring, or brightly colored rubber tiles. Wooden boards needn't be left their natural color: they could be graphically painted with roads, grass shoulders, and rooftops for a car fanatic, or startling purple gloss with yellow planets for a space fan.

Boys still appreciate comfort, so add a thick, cosy rug as well. You could choose a grown-up abstract design in jolly colors that kids will appreciate, too. Some children's online stores or mail-order catalogs stock dual-purpose rugs with parchesi or hopscotch designs, which can be both played with and sat upon. A rug could even be the starting point for a simple decorative theme: a zebra print inspiring a *Jungle Book* mood complete with a fake leopard throw on the bed, or a groovy fake-grass rug for a tractor and barnyard fanatic.

THIS PAGE: **This toddler's bedroom has been created from a sectioned-off area of loft. The plywood storage unit acts as a divider between the room and the living space. Tall ceilings can feel impersonal, but by enclosing the bed with high sides, a cozy corner has been created for a little boy.**

OPPOSITE: **Kids adore sleeping in nooks and crannies, so don't turn the space under the eaves into a closet. A built-in bed might be more fun. Work with the shapes you have: here, a bookcase is part of the design, but extra space might instead be used to create a secret cupboard.**

Though they'll respond instinctively to color and pattern, little guys generally show less interest than girls when asked to select a favorite paint shade or decorative theme. Don't force them: instead, whitewash the walls and inject splashes of contemporary color; anything from a broad-striped scarlet and white quilt cover to a giant orange felt pinboard or lime and indigo denim beanbags. They'll soon tell you if the colors don't suit. If plain walls are too boring, there are plenty of quirky ways to decorate. One wall draped from floor to ceiling with a giant flag looks bold and stylish. Alternatively, line the walls with colorful maps, put up a floor-to-ceiling blackboard for boys to scrawl on, or use metallic silver wallpaper (great as a background for space paintings). Carefully chosen, large props mounted on the wall will also look modern against a single bright color. What about a boogie board, a giant fishing net threaded with plastic fish, or a series of large plastic dinosaurs creeping across the ceiling?

If your little one is mad about a cartoon character, be it Barney or Batman, indulge their passion with a giant floor cushion made in appropriate fabric, or an enormous poster, then ignore further demands. Crazes come and go, and next year your little boy will have moved on to another phase. A generic theme, subtly done, is much more enduring and gives you a decorative "hook" as a starting point. Create a neutral canvas with plain painted walls and a white window shade, then you can introduce all manner of different themes. Kitted out with a green rubber floor, cowhide-patterned furniture, and a blue ceiling, the bedroom becomes a farmyard retreat. With decking, porthole-shaped windows, and a boat-print quilt or bedspread, he'll be at sea exploring every night. Whatever theme you choose, make sure the key elements are inexpensive and easy to change.

THIS PAGE AND OPPOSITE:
A platform bed is a
marvelous spacesaver in a
narrow room. In this seven-
year-old's bedroom, raising
the bed off the ground has
freed up the floor area for
play, and created space for
clothes and toy storage on
each side of the doorway
(above right). The bookcases
are wall hung so do not
impede play space. This
room deftly demonstrates
how to reinterpret the
classic boys' theme—
boats—without covering
everything in motifs. With
its round windows, decking-
effect beech boards, and
metal bed rail, a yacht
springs instantly to mind.

Boys may be boisterous and busy, but there are times when
they want a special area in their bedroom for relaxing and being
with friends. If there's no room for a couch, give your little boy the
chance to turn his bed into a lounge-lizard spot. He will enjoy
touchy-feely fabrics on the bed. Keep bedcovers and sheets in
strong solids (T-shirt jersey bedding is a good texture) and add a
pure wool checked blanket. A giant fleece-fabric blanket in a vivid
hue like scarlet or grass green looks neat tucked over the quilt by
day. A cut-up old sleeping bag, made into squishy cushions, is also
fun. Give boys the chance to create their own ambience in the
room using lighting. A bubble lamp by the bed, a light-up globe on
the desk, or a funky coil of lights are all good options. Try to
squeeze in a few quirky additions. A soccer table game, punchbag,
or wall-hung basketball hoop will make your son's room the
coolest den he could ask for.

" I love climbing up the ladder to go to bed. It's a special place up there."

CHRISTY, AGE 7

shared rooms

Siblings who share need clearly marked personal zones, their own private corners, and decoration they both adore. Kit out their room with two of everything, then create a fun environment that's ideal for shared play and midnight snacks, yet serene enough for soothing bedtimes.

4

Plenty of children share a bedroom. As a parent, you may anticipate only the downsides: disrupted bedtimes, arguments over territory, one child wanting to study while the other chooses to chat. But it needn't be a nightmare. Ask any grown-up who shared a room to recall childhood memories, and many will fondly remember the fun of reading by flashlight after lights-out or the pleasure of two sets of toys. Besides, for a child to wake up with his siblings and fall asleep with them each night is a great gift. Approach decorating a shared bedroom with confidence, and the results will be fun for everyone. Younger siblings may even be fighting to squeeze in.

Demarcation of territory is crucially important. From an early age, children love to have personal space where they can keep their special treasures and retreat with toys or friends. If your kids are small, it's your job to decide who has what space, but with older children include them in the conversation. Start with a floor plan and move around scaled-down cutout pieces of furniture that need to be incorporated to see what works well. If the room has great proportions and two windows, the most sensible option is to split it down the middle. It's more likely that allocating the space will include some compromises, and divisions may not be equal in terms of square feet. Try to compensate fairly. If one child gets the window, give the other the mantelpiece for display.

Kids will find it fun (and you will find it politic) to have a formal division of territory, so that during arguments or when entertaining friends each can retreat to their private zone. First, decide if the division will be visual or physical. For little ones, the less physical

THIS PAGE AND OPPOSITE:
One way to approach a boy-plus-girl shared room is to keep the basics unisex. In this room, shared by a three-year-old girl and seven-year-old boy, polished boards, metal cabinets, and identical beds provide a neutral background. Give each child's area a distinct character by using the bed and wall behind it as a focal point. Paint it hot pink and orange for a girl and muted tones for a boy. Think about the layout: would the kids prefer to sleep at opposite ends of the room or side by side?

THIS PAGE AND OPPOSITE:
An individual wall display by each child's bed is a good way to delineate territory. Here, boldly colored walls are a stunning background for an assortment of objects— tiny dolls' clothes, pictures, photographs, and other treasures. Retro furniture is ideal for kids' rooms. If a piece is not in pristine condition, it doesn't matter if it gets the odd knock, and furniture may come in wild colors with practical, wipe-clean laminated surfaces.

separation the better. They will derive comfort at night by having their beds close together, and reading a joint story will be simpler for you. It might be amusing to divide the room with a brightly painted line of colored footprints or chunky arrows on the wall or on a wooden floor. Older siblings will relish imaginative solutions that section off the bedroom. Consider a plasterboard wall with cutout portholes so the kids can chat, or a floor-to-ceiling sliding screen. Boys might enjoy individual custom-made screens in hole-punched steel that they can wheel to the end of the bed; girls could have four-poster beds draped with voile or organza for privacy.

If your children get along well, divide the room space into separate sleeping, play, and work zones instead of two distinct areas with bed, chest, and so on. This is the most sensible option for older children or if space is restricted. Bunk beds or sleeping pods on a shared platform can be divided from the play space with a sliding screen or floor-to-ceiling sheer curtains. The children can

either share one long countertop to do their homework, or have two identical desks side by side. If older kids find that concentration is a problem, put up a plywood screen between them, and it can double as a pinboard. The remaining floor area can be devoted to fun and games, and there's no further need for a playroom.

When a boy and a girl share, your most pressing problem will be how to marry two definite and probably wildly differing tastes. For little ones, paint the walls white or choose a bold shade, then concentrate on personalizing each child's bed. There's nothing more charming than two identical bedsteads side by side, but characterize each with different bedcovers: an identical design, perhaps, but in contrasting colors. Take the theme a step farther, and color coordinate each child's bedside table, rug, and lampshade. If the children share bunks, individuality is even more essential. Personalize each level with favorite toys and cozy pillows. Alternatively, keep the look coordinated by having differently patterned covers but in harmonizing shades.

When it comes to wall color, older siblings will have fun poring over paint charts to find a hue both can agree on. Provided shades are tonally harmonious, the most extraordinary selection can be combined, and the look will still be confident and modern. For a cohesive scheme, select three shades. Use one for the girl's bedhead wall and another for the boy's headboard wall. A neutral shade works well with brights, so if your daughter wants shocking pink and your son is into army fatigues give him a strong khaki. The third shade can be introduced in the form of upholstery on one side of the room, and picture mats on the other. Painting all four walls in contrasting hues sounds outrageous, but combined with white bedlinen and a wooden floor, it can look fabulous.

Kids' varied tastes in pattern are harder to resolve. A safe bet is to stick to checks, stripes, or dots, but if girls want something floral, an abstract flower-print bedcover will sit well with, for example, a boy's car silhouette. Alternatively, a colorful fantasy mural will appeal to both sexes, but try to keep shapes simple and the look graphic.

" *I love my room because it has my name all over the place. And I love the bookshelf. Now I don't have to keep my books under the bed.* **"**

GEORGIA, AGE 6

THIS PAGE AND OPPOSITE:
In a shared all-girls room,
decorative details can be a
little more indulgent. Both
girls may clamor for pink,
but cooler shades, perhaps
soft blue or faded red, will
still look pretty. If both girls
love the overall scheme,
most elements can be kept
identical. Here, the
symmetry of side-by-side
sleigh beds and twin chairs
creates a tranquil ambience.
Rigorously divide the best
elements of the room: here,
one child has the skylight
while the other gets to turn
off the lamp. Wooden letters
on the wall (opposite) mark
out boundaries.

One neat way to sidestep
the issue of children with
differing tastes is to
dominate a bedroom with a
fabulous mural. Somehow it
negates the need for
boundaries, because the
room becomes a separate
entity, everyone's room, a
magical place to go to sleep
and wake up. A mural is a
clever way to disguise
awkward dimensions: in
Millie, Florence, and
Isabel's bedroom, the tree
shape was inspired by the
chimney breast. Use the
mural to inject an element
of fantasy. Who will care
about sharing a shelf when
everyone can stack books on
a tree branch?

Cool pastels, combined with more boldly colored checks and stripes, are the perfect combination if a girl and boy share, and will appeal to both sexes. The girl's bed can be dressed up with flowers, and the other made more boyish with darker sheets and pillowcases.

Generic themes usually make the best choices simply because they won't date too quickly. Properly painted, a woodland grotto, summer sky, or moonscape can transform a plain bedroom. Remember that kids adore tiny details. Two giant green leaves painted on a white wall and crowded with red and black aphids will keep them amused for many bedtimes. Keep the remaining details simple. Plain, understated window treatments and quilts, simple bedsteads, and contemporary wood or rubber flooring will take the edge off an overly cute visual appeal. Think how you might incorporate imaginative lighting into the mural. Twinkling wall lights emerging from a faux boat mast or starry sky are quite magical for little kids on the brink of sleep.

When same-sex siblings are sharing, you can easily indulge all-girl fantasies or all-boy passions. But you still need to personalize the two-of-everything accessories, so that sharers are clear about who owns what. You might want to keep the theme subtle with color coding: pink for one child's furniture and toy boxes, green for the other's. Bedding, laundry bags, lampshades, and slipcovered chairs can all be individualized with a giant monogram, or allot each child a motif—perhaps a car for one, a butterfly for the other—which each can easily recognize as his or her own. Individual display areas, for everything from stones from the beach to photographs or framed certificates, and a section of wall or pinboard for personal artwork, are absolutely essential.

66 *My sister Sophie and I talk after lights-out and plot midnight snacks.* 99

JACK, AGE 7

THIS PAGE: Two studio beds placed at right angles, with a shared, sturdy cube side table, is a comforting and sensible option for little children. For Molly and Eli, there is no danger of knocking over furniture, and they can chat in bed while retaining a little privacy. In a shared room, good storage is essential, so consider below-bed toy drawers and low studio beds that can double as a daytime sofa. OPPOSITE: Sharing a bedroom is about fun, so it's a sound investment to custom-build a giant platform that can sleep two, or hold one mattress with a play area at the other end.

Some children are messy, while others are very neat, so to avoid arguments over clearing up, give each child his or her own chest of drawers, shelves, or closet. A bedside table for each, to hold a nighttime drink, books, and lamp, is also essential. Don't attempt to separate toy storage: if children are sharing a bedroom, then it makes sense for toys to be communal. It's a good idea to provide a few crates with lids for each child, however, so special toys like Barbie dolls or Pokémon cards can be kept well out of the way of inquisitive small siblings. Because a shared bedroom frequently doubles as a playroom, make sure everything can be cleared away quickly and hidden behind closed doors. Bedtime with two excitable children is stressful enough without a jumble of tempting toys peeping out from wicker baskets.

If you've picked a stimulating decorative scheme, flexible lighting is one way to calm things down at bedtime. In shared rooms, the correct lighting becomes even more important. Different-aged children may have staggered lights-out times, so while an older child needs a well-shaded task light for reading in bed, his younger sibling might require a glowing nightlight. For playtime, low-voltage ceiling lights give brighter illumination than a single overhead fixture, but install a dimmer switch for nighttime. Consider a wacky lighting feature that both kids will enjoy. A giant clock, light-projected onto the wall, or an illuminated fish tank, would both look stunning.

When children enjoy sharing a bedroom, it becomes a real den, their own private space versus the family house, and a brilliant place to chill out. If space permits, give them a daybed, a child-size chaise longue, or an inflatable chair to lounge on, and consider installing a TV for older kids. If there is a younger sibling who doesn't share, and everyone is in agreement, the daybed (or rollaway) could be used at weekends for sleepovers so the little one can join in the fun. Likewise, give each child who shares the chance to sleep alone occasionally, in a spare bedroom or on a convertible sofa. Children, like adults, occasionally need time out from the fray.

THIS PAGE AND OPPOSITE: Offered the chance of bunk beds, most brothers will jump at the chance of sharing, though you can expect inevitable arguments about who gets the top bunk. This room for older boys takes a shared dormitory as its theme. White shutters, no-nonsense floorboards, and utilitarian metal-framed beds all suggest summer camp, while the furniture— a battered footlocker, individual initialed trunks, and aluminum chairs— completes the look. If dorm-style is your chosen theme, shared clothes storage and identical bedding are all part of the fun.

" *I like sharing. But Bo*

kicks my bed! "

Plan a practical yet imaginative bathroom so the kids' daily ablutions are fun. Aim for a family bathroom that's sophisticated enough for grown-ups, but suitable for children, too. Flexible storage and neutral shades are the keys to success.

bath  rooms

5

The bathroom is one of the most hard-working spaces in the house. It needs to be efficient enough for the before-school wash and brush-up, yet cozy enough to prompt fun-filled bathtimes. In terms of encouraging washing routines, you've won half the battle if the bathroom is a tempting place to spend time. Most children have a love–hate relationship with their daily ablutions. One week, they will obsessively brush their teeth; the next, they're terrified of the shower. But nearly all little ones find bathing soothing. Around the age of seven, children may choose not to bathe with siblings. Girls prefer splashing around with lotions and potions, while boys would rather be anywhere than in the bathroom.

If it's possible, give the children their own bathroom, which can also be used by guests. A designated kids' bathroom means you can install splashproof materials, scaled-down sanitaryware, and jolly colors, and save more sophisticated details for your own bathroom. But if the room is really tiny, consider other options. Would you be better off creating a family-size bathroom elsewhere, with space for a large tub plus comfy chair? Would the tiny room work better with a toilet and basin, rather than trying to squeeze in a tub as well? Depending on the layout of the house, it might make sense for you to sacrifice your planned bathroom to the family and have a tiny connecting shower room instead. Site the kids' bathroom close to their bedrooms. Slippery tired children make bathtime chaotic enough, so the nearer they are to their pajamas, the better.

If you're planning a bathroom from scratch, first decide whether to have a bathtub and separate shower cubicle, or a wall-mounted shower attachment over the bathtub. Little ones generally prefer baths to showers. Many find the pressure of a power shower uncomfortable on their heads, and they may be frightened by the sheer volume of rushing water.

THIS PAGE AND OPPOSITE: A shared family bathroom has to please everyone, and with its zingy grapefruit color scheme and glass skylights, this one does the trick. Always devote as much space as possible to the bathroom, then combine with an invigorating color scheme and lots of light.

Good storage is essential, too. In this bathroom, there are under-sink cupboards as well as out-of-reach units for grown-up toiletries. The double sinks are ideal for the morning rush. Adding a built-in diaper changing area is a nifty idea, but put shelving for the equipment within arm's reach.

THIS PAGE AND OPPOSITE: Bathtime is much more fun for kids if there are decorative touches that appeal to their imagination. But if a bathroom is shared with adults, you can't allow kids' stuff to take over. The answer is to keep the decor plain, using white tiles or tongue-and-groove paneling, so that the style easily reverts to a grown-up mood. Essential details include a waterproof toy basket and low shelves for the children's bubblebath. A wacky shower curtain is a great way to inject fun: shimmery silver, 3D flowers, or pockets for family snapshots are all good. Any extras will be appreciated, from a funky bathroom cabinet to a fish tank.

THIS PAGE AND OPPOSITE:

In a kids-only bathroom, installing a small low-level bathtub and mini-washbasin is an appealing option. Roll-top tubs are especially appropriate for children, as there are no sharp edges to bang little heads on.

Reconditioned Victorian bathtubs are often a good option, as many come in small sizes. Consider having a central tub: it makes getting in and out easier, and there is also less likelihood of the walls getting splashed.

Children love to be independent, and being able to climb in and out of the tub by themselves is a milestone. But if the children's bathroom is to be shared with guests, spare a thought for an adult trying to squeeze into a tiny tub, and think twice before choosing a low, small version.

However, children are more likely to slip if they shower standing up in a tub. If an over-the-bath shower is the only option, buy a nonslip rubber mat and a plastic shower curtain. Probably the best configuration is to site a grown-up shower elsewhere in the house, and equip the children's bathtub with a hand-held shower attachment for washing hair.

Children love to be independent, and being able to climb in and out of the tub by themselves is a milestone. But if the children's bathroom is to be shared with guests, spare a thought for an adult trying to squeeze into a tiny tub and think twice before choosing a low, small version. A big bathtub has lots of advantages. When siblings bathe together, they appreciate plenty of space for play, while in a family bathroom a generous tub will give you a share of adult luxury. Remember, putting the faucet in the center means neither child has to have the faucet end.

To cope with the early morning rush, two (or even three) basins make sense. A row of scaled-down basins looks eye-catching, and is a sensible option if space is tight. There are plenty of stylish, practical choices that are ideal for kids. Small stainless-steel bowls set into a stone or wood counter look ultra-trendy, as do wall-hung white ceramic sinks. A specially designed small basin is another option. The appeal of a wall-hung or inset basin is that you can lower the height for kids. For standard-size pedestal sinks, provide a sturdy stool so children can step up to the correct height.

Little details will give small children the confidence they need to use the bathroom alone. X-shaped or lever faucets are much easier to handle than slippery, minimal round knobs, while a temperature control will help guard against scalds. Wall-mounted faucets are easier to keep clean than ones on the sink. A counter with an inset washbasin provides ample space for washroom essentials. But if the basin is freestanding, put a toothbrush holder on the wall, so it can't be knocked over, and replace slippery soap bars with liquid soap in a neat chrome dispenser. Think about the toilet. A wall-hung model can be sited slightly lower down. Is the handle too stiff for little fingers to flush? Would a push-button mechanism be better? If you have room, install a generously sized heated towel rod. There's nothing worse than being enfolded in yesterday's damp towel.

Make your bathroom one hundred percent splashproof now, and you won't mind about water fights later. Fun floor options include nonslip rubber tiles in bright colors as well as linoleum and vinyl. Cork floor tiles with laminate finish also come in water-themed designs such as sand and shells. Sealed or painted wooden boards are also suitable, though wood laminates are sensitive to deluges of bathwater. Stone, such as limestone or slate, is stylish, waterproof and, if you install underfloor heating, feels fabulous underfoot. However, it does get slippery when wet, so invest in a cozy absorbent bathmat. Children will also adore a concrete floor studded with pebbles and little shells, which also has plenty of grip.

The walls will get splashed with lots of water, so floor-to-ceiling tiles are sensible. In a kids-only bathroom, big square tiles in a cheerful shade look graphic and modern. For a coordinated look, color-match them with

OPPOSITE, LEFT: **Small details, such as a colorful toilet seat, can transform an all-white bathroom.**

OPPOSITE, RIGHT: **Surfaces must be robust and easy to clean. Vividly colored laminates make good paneling, while stone, from slate to marble, is practical as well as stylish.**

THIS PAGE: **The ultimate luxury of a kids-only bathroom is that sinks can be situated at child height. Don't forget to include a stool for adults to perch on while supervising bathtime.**

THIS PAGE: In a bathroom shared by adults and kids, a deep bathtub adds a sense of luxury and is great to wallow in. If planning a shower, install an oversized shower tray, or build a "wet" shower, so all the kids can squeeze in together. If you install a power shower, choose a showerhead with the option for gentler spray.

OPPOSITE: If space allows, double basins make perfect sense in a shared bathroom. Provide steps so little ones, like five-year-old Gussie, can reach the basin. Allocate one basin to the children, with a shelf for toothbrushes and novelty soaps, then gather more sophisticated "grown-up" toiletries around the other.

a painted wooden floor or laminated counters. In a shared family bathroom, subway-style white brick tiles create a more sophisticated look, but work just as well with colorful bath toys as with adult accessories. Limestone-covered walls are another grown-up option, but resist glass and stainless-steel splashbacks. They may look chic, but will show every water mark. Laminates, which come in a host of enticing colors, are another good choice for paneling and cabinet doors.

Walls can also be lined with tongue-and-groove or board panels. Paint them and the walls eggshell, which resists splash marks and condensation well. If sanitaryware is white, have fun with color on the walls. Jazzy shades such as grass green and turquoise are particularly appropriate. Paint broad horizontal stripes on walls or use color to delineate different doors on built-in cabinets. In a shared family bathroom, you need to design a chameleonlike color scheme. The combination of a sophisticated surface like limestone with a restful palette of taupe, lilac, or eau-de-nil guarantees a bathroom that's grown-up when the kids' things are put away, yet is still an appropriate backdrop for plastic bath toys. Steer kids away from garish novelty character towels, and provide plain ones that complement the rest of the room.

Plan plenty of storage for bathroom paraphernalia, including a high lockable cabinet for any medicines. In a shared family bathroom, give the kids a place for novelty bubblebaths and soaps. You won't have to share your grown-up soak with a jumble of bottles, and surfaces are easier to keep clean when free of toiletries. The same principle applies to toys: provide a big plastic box, and after bathtime they can be put away so the space looks sophisticated again. In a kids-only bathroom, display plastic fish and submarines on shelves above the tub.

play spaces

Play—be it energetic, be it peaceful—is the centralizing force in a child's life, so kids need space to scoot around and spread their toys in. Grown-ups need to be able to clear it all away. Storage that works is the key.

6

THIS PAGE AND OPPOSITE: With forethought, a great play space can be seamlessly integrated into an open-plan living and kitchen area. Modern flooring materials like limestone and concrete are perfect surfaces for toy trains and cars, and, with underfloor heating, are warm and comfortable to play on. If planning a play space from scratch, doors to an outside space are a worthwhile investment. They let in light and increase the play space when open. Add streamlined and unobtrusive storage. In Pablo's play space, roomy sliding drawers give him easy access to his toys.

66 *This is a really big space for my trains. I like playing here so I'm next to Mommy when she's in the kitchen.* **99**

PABLO, AGE 3 ½

Every child needs space to play. An expanse of floor, a freshly cleared tabletop, and enough room to race around are the essentials—without these, children have no free rein with their toys. As adults, we allocate ourselves activity zones: a sofa to sprawl on, a desk for paying bills, an armchair for reading. Children need their own equivalent. It's not fair to tell children they can play all over the house, only to scold them for piling toys on the stairs. Try to give your kids a special area where they know they can play. Size isn't the issue—whether it's a patch of floor within a kitchen/dining room, or a separate playroom, what's important is that this is a space they can call their own. Make toys accessible and easy to put away, and kids will even enjoy organizing their own private zone.

In recent years, many families have devoted their largest living space to a kitchen, dining, and playroom all rolled into one. In a conventional house or apartment, an open-plan area is easily created by knocking down walls. But loft conversions are increasingly on the agenda. A decade ago, lofts were the province of the trendy and the child-free. But those same couples are now having families and enjoying the benefits of a vast one-level floor space. A loft or warehouse space creates the ultimate indoor playground, with ample room for bike-riding and space-hopping.

The advantages of an open-plan living space are manifold. Tiny children can play under a grown-up's watchful eye, while cooking, video-watching, and older kids' homework all get under way. If you're moving to accommodate a growing family, this is the ideal space configuration. It's helpful to have a toilet nearby, so little ones don't have to travel too far. And, if possible, access from the living area/play space to a backyard or roof terrace is invaluable. In summer, it doubles the available floor area, while in winter the kids might be more easily tempted outdoors.

If you can't move, but are adapting your living quarters to accommodate children, think long and hard about the changes you make. You will reap the benefits of employing an architect, although it may seem a major investment at the time. An architect will think more laterally about maximizing space and can squeeze storage into the most unlikely corners. Alternatively, if finances are tight, can rooms be swapped around? Perhaps a dining room off the kitchen could be converted into a playroom, or an underused sunroom adapted into a kids' den? However, if you have a spare room away from the living area that you might convert into a separate playroom, think twice about doing so when your children are small. You won't want to be cooking with half an ear on what's going on next door, and life is infinitely easier if you don't have to call a halt to exciting play in one room and move children to the kitchen to eat. Far better to include the kids' play area within the bosom of the house and get on with the riotous business of family life.

The area chosen for a play space needs to provide a decent amount of floor area for spreading out toys as well as enough room to run around. Make sure everything else going on in the same space won't interfere with the kids' activities, and vice versa. Could you re-route traffic through a play area by moving a sofa to one side of the room? Will you be forever tripping over toddlers while trying to prepare food? If the play space is within or adjacent to the kitchen, safety is vital. Clip trailing wires and cushion sharp corners. Install child locks on cabinets and put safety covers on sockets, and always, always, tuck in saucepan handles.

The downside of sharing a living space with children is that they bring a sea of brightly colored plastic with them. It's natural to worry that their arrival may cramp your style-conscious home, yet a minimal interior

" It was a way to prevent toys cluttering up the floor. " FRIEDA, MOTHER

THIS PAGE AND OPPOSITE: While lofts and kids mix well, as there's so much open space it helps adults and children to be neat if one area is designated as the toy zone. Where there is a very large floor area, building a child-height maze from painted partitions makes good sense, as Juliet and Lucie's parents found out. Make it big enough to hold several little "rooms" where toy stores or doll houses can be permanently located. Painted a strong color and set amid white walls, the maze will become a talking point among adults and a magnet for kids.

needn't disappear forever. Rule number one is to provide effective storage so that in the evenings toys can be put away quickly and easily and grown-up order restored. The best solution is to kit out your living/play space with floor-to-ceiling closets with flush doors and deep shelves. Locate the kids' things on the lower shelves and use the upper ones for household paraphernalia. If you can, specify extra-deep shelves so fold-up dolls' buggies or plastic garages can fit in easily. If there's no room for a closet, and open shelves are the only option, invest in some decent-looking containers that look good *en masse*. Clear plastic crates and wicker baskets are both practical and stylish.

Rule number two is that precious or beautiful pieces should be put into storage or placed firmly out of reach. If you have the luxury of a grown-ups-only living room, then enjoy them in there. It's easy to teach children to respect lovely things and not to draw on the walls, but sensible to accept that accidents will happen. So protect your cherrywood dining table with a wipe-clean cloth and your expensively upholstered sofa with a slipcover in a tough, washable fabric. Replace a limited-edition rug with an abstract one from a chain store. Beaded pillows, velvet throws, or anything else labeled "dry-clean-only" should be removed. Remember, you're creating a child-friendly zone so that everyone can relax.

If you've moved, decorating and furnishing a play space that doubles as a family living room is great fun. The beauty of integrating kids' stuff with contemporary design is that trendy industrial-style surfaces like stainless steel, plywood, and laminate are stylish and hard-wearing, and the clear, bright colors of much modern furniture are enhanced when it is littered with toys. When you are decorating walls, white flat vinyl latex creates a simple background, and scuff marks are easily touched up.

OPPOSITE ABOVE: **Every play space needs comfortable, low-level seating for chilling out in front of the video or reading. A simple bench with comfy cushions, like this one, can incorporate narrow drawers for small toys and jigsaws.**
OPPOSITE BELOW: **As an alternative to the ubiquitous miniature table and chairs, a wooden desktop, set on an adjustable rack system, provides a corner for quiet play or drawing and writing, and can grow with the child.**
LEFT: **In a large living room, try to incorporate desk space for older children, for homework, coloring, or for the family computer.**

play spaces **95**

PREVIOUS PAGES: **With a little** judicious selection, there are plenty of playful features that remain easy on the eye when they are installed in a sophisticated adult space. The key is to use them with confidence, scale them up, and choose colors that will positively enhance the grown-up scheme. Thus, a blackboard can take up half the wall (useful for shopping lists or phone messages), and beanbags can be adult-size and stylish, perhaps in leather or vinyl. Appropriately placed, a toy such as a bright red child's swing, suspended from the ceiling, can have as much decorative impact as a contemporary chair.

THIS PAGE AND OPPOSITE: If space and your budget allow, a child-size heated indoor swimming pool provides kids with the ultimate play space and, if equipped with a swimming current for adults, can be used by the whole family. The parents of these children have positioned a big, comfortable sofa beyond the splashproof glass doors, so an adult can supervise in comfort.

But have fun with color, too. A single wall painted vibrant lime green or dazzling bright blue can look stunning, particularly if it is decorated with children's artwork, properly framed and displayed.

Practical furniture makes life much easier. Polypropylene chairs are a sensible, easy-clean option, and 1960s-style versions in vivid tangerine and lime green are great fun. If a table doubles as a dining and painting table, a wipe-clean surface is essential, so a cement or laminated top is ideal. If the table needs to be pushed to one side to create a more flexible space, add castors and the look becomes trendier still. To house the video, choose a long cabinet instead of open shelves. Have a steel one powder-coated in shocking pink, and make a design statement at the same time.

You can be similarly imaginative when selecting fabric for the playroom sofa or chairs. Several bright solids can look stunningly abstract used as blocks of color on individual chairs, seats, and cushions. Leather is durable and stylish as well as ultra-practical because it can be wiped clean. Patterned fabric is excellent for disguising sticky finger marks. Find something bold and wacky that will appeal to both you and the kids: giant cabbage roses on a slim steel-legged sofa, or a 1950s pictorial print of seaside scenes. When it comes to decorating a play space, you can be a little tongue-in-cheek. A 1970s swivel chair upholstered in Mr. Men fabric would look funky, as might a giant abstract painting that blurs the barriers between modern art and kids' naïve efforts.

Every play space needs a cozy corner for watching a video or listening to music. If space permits, a small sofa is great for after-lunch naps or quiet reading; if there's no room, beanbags work equally well. Play spaces in communal living areas often have hard floors, perhaps wood or limestone, so a rug or a fluffy faux animal-print throw provides a softer sitting or crawling area for babies and toddlers. Keep the television out of the way by mounting it on a wall bracket or a pull-out arm concealed in a cabinet. But try to site the video at child level, as even two-year-olds will relish the independence of slotting in their favorite film. Provide plenty of storage for videos nearby. They can be fitted into mini plastic crates or stacked in a narrow section of custom-made shelving. If you're blessed with abundant living space, you can include a few wacky extras. Consider hanging a swing from the ceiling, or keeping a pop-up tent or play house permanently erected.

OPPOSITE ABOVE LEFT AND RIGHT, AND BELOW RIGHT: **Kids glory in the luxury of plenty of play space, yet the adults haven't been forced to compromise their space in these three homes. The modern classic furniture, contemporary sofas in bright colors, and casual floor cushions, are as trendy as they are child-friendly, so everyone benefits.**

OPPOSITE BELOW LEFT: **A sophisticated adult living room can still be family-oriented with sensible choices like washable covers and stain-guarded upholstery. Molly and Eli have soon learned what they can and can't touch.**

OPPOSITE BELOW RIGHT: **When a living room doubles as a play space, there must be plenty of storage for quick clear-ups. Nica stuffs toys into the retro sideboard and 1970s stacking compartments. Graphic, colorful art will appeal to adults and children alike.**

OPPOSITE: With their vast expanses of floor space, city lofts are wonderful for urban children. There's even room to ride a bike, so on rainy days, kids can burn off exercise at home. Johanna's parents have a side sitting area where they can relax while watching the children. THIS PAGE: A long, comfortable sofa, big enough for the whole family, makes an ideal centerpiece, but for practicality stick with strong colored upholstery or a busy pattern to conceal spills and stains.

spaces to # eat

Little ones need a calm and comfortable spot for eating beneath your watchful gaze. Choose wipe-clean furniture and scaled-down shapes, with plates and flatware in jelly-bean shades, and you'll tempt even the most reluctant eater to the table.

7

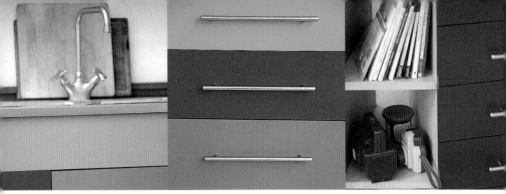

These days, it's common for children to gather in the kitchen, so if you're planning a new one make it a stimulating place to be. This example was deliberately designed with small children in mind. Ease of use is paramount. The long bar handles are simple for kids to grab, and their plates and cups are located in a low drawer. Island units make sense: children can gather around and help cook, eat meals there, or sit and draw. Plan plenty of drawers, so that napkins, straws, and placemats are easy for kids to reach.

Kids' mealtimes may seem like lunchtime at the zoo, but if you choose practical yet good-looking furniture and equipment at least cleaning up will take zero time. In the early years, babies progress rapidly from being spoon-fed to helping themselves in a highchair, then graduating to the grown-ups' table. Whatever stage they're at, the process of getting kids to sit down, eat calmly, and observe table manners needs to be achieved with minimum fuss and maximum efficiency. If there is a comfortable eating area and food is presented attractively, recalcitrant eaters are more likely to hop up to the table.

If possible, situate the table in the kitchen, so you can keep an eye on the kids while you prepare food or clear up. The advantages are obvious—you're on the spot if a child chokes, the kitchen floor is practical and wipe-clean, and food, drink, and a damp cloth for sticky faces are all close at hand. Don't despair that your high-tech modern kitchen will be spoiled by highchairs and bright dishes. Source attractive furniture and kitchenware, and the transition will be seamless. Colorful seating, a lime-green toaster, or pink plastic glasses will only pep up a stainless-steel kitchen.

It's fun to provide little ones with a diminutive table and chairs at which they can eat meals or draw and paint. Good-looking styles include miniature versions of the classic Arne Jacobsen "Ant" chair.

A highchair is essential for babies. Standard designs are practical, but often rather an eyesore. You can either accept this and put up with it, or find a more attractive option. There are simple wooden Scandinavian designs available, or plain white lacquered steel versions. Alternatively, look for a secondhand highchair. Repaint it a bold color and re-cover the seat in a retro-print oilcloth. You may need to add new safety straps.

If you have older children who eat at the main table, a sturdy canvas or plastic clip-on seat is sociable for older babies, because it attaches to the tabletop. You might also consider a highchair designed to grow with the child. These often come in stylish chrome and beech. They feature a clip-on tray and safety guard for the baby stage, then adapt, leaving just a useful footrest, into a seat for older children.

THIS PAGE AND OPPOSITE: It's nice to give children the option of eating at the dining table or at their own special miniature table. Choose a big family table, so there's always room for friends, and select a tough tabletop to withstand spills and scratches. Good materials include zinc, stainless steel, cement, marble, slate, or laminate. Save the designer chairs for later years. For a growing family, it's more fun to have mismatched wooden chairs, painted in fun colors, or comfortably upholstered ones with washable covers.

THIS PAGE AND OPPOSITE: It makes sense to think of the children's plates and flatware as an extension of the adults' options, so the table looks coordinated. Scour stores for trendy, informal tableware that everyone can share: jewel-colored glasses, hand-painted bowls (this page), and chunky ceramic mugs (opposite below right), ideal for both milk or a cup of coffee. Here, Harry enjoys his cereal from a small bowl (opposite below center)). Children love pottery-painting cafés, where they can decorate their very own cups and plates. And buying a picnic set with jolly colored plates and bowls has a dual function: the kids can use it both on a day-to-day basis as well as for family outings.

It's fun to provide little ones with a diminutive table and chairs at which they can eat meals or draw and paint. However, if you like to sit with the kids while they eat, you may not find it such a comfortable option. Eating at a breakfast bar or adding a low countertop to the end of an island unit might be a more casual, user-friendly solution. The choice of small-scale tables and chairs has increased recently; look in chain stores, kids' catalogs, or grown-up contemporary design emporia. It's also worth investigating nursery furniture designed for schools. Good-looking styles include miniature versions of the classic Arne Jacobsen "Ant" chair, chunky wooden seats in primary colors, or whitewashed Swedish-style tables and benches. You can match the style to your kitchen.

The sooner you encourage small children to sit at the grown-ups' table, the better; it socializes them, and fosters a sense of independence. If you have a beautiful table, protect it with a plastic cloth at all times. The same goes for upholstered dining chairs: it may sound like an investment to have a set of slipcovers made, but the upholstery will be saved from sticky fingers. If you are choosing new chairs for family mealtimes, look for

Retro highchairs are by far the most tasteful versions on offer. Scour secondhand stores for old wooden models that can be enlivened with paint or a new laminated tray. Choose a style to harmonize with the other chairs around the table, so that baby can join in stylishly at mealtimes!

polypropylene, metal, or wood. Light chairs in plastic or aluminum are good, because a small child can maneuver one by himself. Pick a style that is comfortable for kids as well as looking chic. A slatted seat can trap fingers, while a chair with arms won't pull close enough to the table for a small person to eat in comfort. School-style benches are also excellent, providing plenty of extra room for friends. High stools at a breakfast bar are great for older children, but make sure little ones won't overbalance.

With imaginative shopping, you and the kids will find setting the table positively creative. Tiny versions of anything will delight them, and a choice of colors is great, because each can pick their favorite shade. Not everything has to be plastic, although picnic sets in dayglo colors are a good source of plates and cups. Duralex glasses are virtually indestructible and come in appealingly small

sizes. Many casual dining sets are robust pottery, and traditional enamel plates and cups are also hard-wearing. These days, many manufacturers produce bright-handled flatware in small sizes. Customize placemats: draw on slate slabs with chalks or transfer a favorite photograph onto mats. Alternatively, scour art and design supply stores for wacky wipe-clean placemats and pictorial napkins.

Everything to do with kids' mealtimes should be accessible for them, as it encourages setting the table from an early age. Store bowls and flatware in a low cabinet or drawer and keep lunchboxes there, too. Is the refrigerator easy for an older child to open, so they can help themselves to snacks? Is there a sturdy stepstool for a little one to hop on so he can get a drink of water from the sink? The easier you make eating and drinking for your children, the sooner they will be integrated into the sociable world of family mealtimes.

ABOVE LEFT AND RIGHT: **Miniature table and chair sets needn't be clumsy pieces of molded plastic in garish colors. For an individual and stylish look, choose more elegant versions that mimic grown-up contemporary styles, such as these little molded beech-veneer 1960s-style chairs (above left).**

Call it paraphernalia, equipment, toys, or simply stuff, children have an alarming number of possessions. If the whole family is to enjoy a peaceful and efficient living space, it's up to you to squeeze great storage out of every square inch.

spaces for storage

8

THIS PAGE: **When a bedroom is also a playroom, closet doors that conceal toys will guarantee more restful bedtimes. In this loft, plexiglass and plywood are used throughout, not just in the child's room.**

OPPOSITE: **Capacious toy drawers hold lots and are easy for children to reach. Be imaginative with the drawer fronts: cut out patterns in the front or choose stainless-steel or painted wood fascias.**

New parents soon learn that children come complete with lots of stuff. Over the years, regular clear-outs will help, but the fact remains that the minute you start a family your need for hard-working storage increases tenfold. After the baby bouncer and sit-on fire engine come fleets of tiny cars and dolls' accessories, then homemade models, musical instruments, tennis rackets, and more. Accept the influx with good grace, and set about planning where everything should go. It's a cliché, but a place for everything is the ultimate aim, even if frenetic family life doesn't allow for an "everything in its place" conclusion.

However capacious the storage in the kids' bedrooms and play space, there will be yet more stuff you need to house in heavy traffic areas like the hall. Ask yourself where outdoor gear—coats, hats, umbrellas, boots, and strollers—will go. What about sports equipment—ballet and swimming bags, footballs, and baseball bats? The older children get, the bigger their kit becomes. Bikes need a home, as do tents, sleeping bags, and outdoor games.

If there is room in your hall, a large built-in closet will hold all the essentials and keep things neat. Be sure to leave room for shoe storage. For small children, a low row of hooks on the wall is better: outdoor gear can be seen at a glance, and little ones may be more inclined to hang up their bags. Use a big basket or galvanized metal tub to hold shoes, and another for hats, scarves, and gloves. A low bench where children can perch while doing up their shoes should be situated near the coat rack. Pick one with a lift-up lid and extra storage within. If bikes are a problem and the hall is high enough, fit them onto a wall rack. Alternatively, store them in the backyard or a shed or garage.

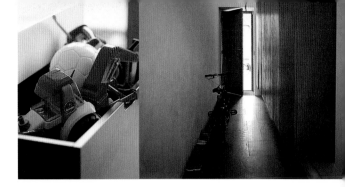

PREVIOUS PAGE: **Large drawers and deep shelves are essential for storing toys, but just as crucial is plenty of individual containers. They allow kids to organize their toys, so there are homes for pens, plastic animals, blocks, books, toy cars, and so on. Anything can be used as a container, from galvanized metal buckets to sisal baskets. See-at-a-glance storage is the most helpful, so choose open-topped baskets, transparent plastic crates, or screw-topped jars. Label everything, so everyone knows what goes where.**
ABOVE RIGHT: **If you're planning a family home from scratch, a separate corridor running along the side of the house can be devoted to bikes, outdoor gear, and sports equipment. Here, closets create a spacious effect.**
OPPOSITE: **Even in a small hall, provide a child-sized stool or bench so kids can sit down and pull their boots and shoes on and off.**

In long, narrow halls, there's space for little more than a row of coat hooks and an umbrella stand. Storage must be squeezed in elsewhere—perhaps in a cupboard under the stairs, or incorporated into shelves or cabinets in the play area. Don't expect everyday gear to be stored in the children's bedrooms. You need everything on hand for the early-morning rush. However, an array of hanging bags and coats will look messy in an open-plan living and play area. A smart solution is to build a grid system of shelves, each just big enough to hold a labeled wicker basket, and pack everything in. Perhaps a cupboard in the utility room could hold outdoor gear, while open shelves by the back door are good for shoe storage.

In the kitchen/living/play space, it's essential that you and the kids have enough storage for day-to-day paraphernalia so everyone stays organized. Display the school calendar, reading lists, and sports schedules on a giant pinboard, and if its messy appearance spoils a chic dining area, hang it inside a closet door. If the play zone is part of the kitchen, clear a kitchen cabinet or drawer so barettes and brushes, museum pamphlets, painting equipment, and Play-Doh are easily cleared up, yet can be just as easily found

THIS PAGE AND OPPOSITE: Tailor-made storage may seem like an indulgence, but it makes daily activities like changing diapers and getting the kids dressed much simpler. Lots of little compartments are the key to good organization. List the things to be stored, from cotton balls to baby undershirts, then provide well-regimented cubbyholes. Stack see-at-a-glance glass-fronted cabinets with open-topped storage boxes, line a shelf with wicker baskets, or make a decorative feature out of labeling individual drawers. Customize wherever possible: if a cabinet lacks enough compartments, then add your own divisions.

when needed. If you are planning a kitchen from scratch, consider choosing a central island unit with drawers and cabinets that can be devoted to stashing away your children's clutter.

Built-in storage needs to look fabulous as well as being practical—so design it as an integral part of your decorating scheme, not as an afterthought. If you have one baby now, double the storage you've planned because it will all be used eventually. For the neatest look, cover all your shelves with doors. They can be wide and sliding or narrow and flush, with finishes in everything from painted board to sand-blasted glass, zinc, plastic, or wood. Avoid open shelves: lovely as they look when just built, the clean, clutter-free look will be gone once they are crammed with toys, books, and equipment. Use every spare inch of space. Floor-level drawers are great for toys, while a narrow alcove can hold bookshelves. There's still a place for freestanding furniture, but go for quirky pieces that add character, like an old metal school locker.

There's no point in having good storage if children won't use it. Make it so simple for them that there can be no arguments. Handles should be easy to grip, so look for metal D-handles, recessed door pulls, and chunky knobs. Keep some shelves shallow, so items don't get lost at the back. Within a closet, divide up paper, pens, scissors, and glues within small plastic crates, sisal baskets, or good old-fashioned tin cans. Compartmentalize drawers with readymade dividers or make your own. And label boxes and crates. If your children can't read yet, use a picture of each toy type for reference, or color code things: red for books, blue for cars and so on. When one activity is finished, teach the kids to put everything away before they start the next game. It's a lesson we adults could do well to learn, too!

Kids love outdoor spaces, where they can run, jump, and play crazy games. Give them a secret hideaway and they'll disappear for hours. It doesn't matter whether you have a modest city yard or a huge lawn—any outdoor space allows children to let off steam.

outdoor spaces

9

Let children loose in an open space and they're off, tearing about with all the delight of a puppy off the leash. If properly wrapped up, they rarely notice if it's cold and the grass is wet, and on a summer's day will happily stay outdoors till dusk. Try to give them some outside space. We can't all have vast lawns, but even a tiny backyard or roof terrace has potential for creative play.

Design's current obsession with the indoor–outdoor principle has many benefits for children and is the perfect solution in a small urban patch. A play space that opens straight into the backyard makes outdoors very accessible. Children can run in and out, and are easily visible to adults within. If your property doesn't allow for this arrangement, consider the exit points from the house. Ideally, kids should be able to get in and out by themselves, so French or sliding doors are ideal. If the only access to the outside is through a "precious" adult living room with a carpeted floor, could you create a new door, perhaps via a utility room or the kitchen?

THIS PAGE AND OPPOSITE: A sunroom playroom gives the best of both worlds: in Lucy and Sisi's, the door can be thrown open on sunny days, and they get the benefit of lots of daylight, even in winter. Shades are a must, to guard against glare and keep the room cool. A sunroom playroom needs robust, weatherproof furniture, so that it isn't a disaster if a chair is left outside overnight, and should also provide storage for outdoor play equipment.

THIS PAGE AND OPPOSITE: **Nothing beats the appeal of an outdoor playhouse. It's relatively simple to adapt a readymade wooden shed, customizing it with a "gingerbread" roof trim or a stable-style door. Make sure the playhouse is waterproof, then help your children decorate the inside, perhaps with a painted wooden floor or even wallpaper. For real imaginative play, the house must have a window and a door. Fit in chairs and a table, and supply galvanized metal tubs or wicker baskets for chucking toys into at the end of the day.**

The whole point about children playing outside is that they should be able to do so unaccompanied—it's no fun playing cowboys and Indians with a grown-up standing by. Tiny ones do need more of a watchful eye. Before you let them loose, make sure children will be absolutely safe. Put a lock on the back gate and make sure they can't climb over the fence or fall over the edge of a roof terrace. Are all swings, ropes, and treehouse ladders secure and well-supported? Water features, from a tiny pond to a swimming pool, must be made child-safe, too. Somehow, you need to make the kids feel free, while still keeping a close watch on what they're up to. One option is to create a screen separating a children's play area at one end of the yard from the rest of the lawn. Construct it from large-scale trellis or bamboo, so you can see through the gaps. And a treehouse should be visible from at least one window in the house.

A playhouse is always a winner. Children love the idea of a private space of their own, and they can store all their outside toys there. There's no need to spoil your yard with a garish plastic structure: the wooden variety is much more tasteful. However, custom-made children's cottages can be ruinously expensive. Far better to design your own and get a carpenter to make it, or even to adapt an ordinary garden shed. So long as the structure has a door and windows, it will be heaven for little girls and boys. Reach a stylistic compromise on the decoration. If you choose to paint the exterior a subtle color like lichen green, allow the kids to design the inside. Staple-gun fabric remnants to the inside of windows for curtains, and add little chairs and tables. If budget permits, a more

sophisticated playhouse can be equipped with water, electricity, and heating. It could even double as a home office or guest room.

A treehouse or raised platform between branches will double the appeal of being outdoors. You could make it to scaled-down proportions, so that only kids can squeeze through the opening into their "house". Alternatively, build it big enough for the whole family to enjoy an evening meal up there. Apart from ladders, all sorts of extras can be added. Suspend a hammock, hang a string of Chinese lanterns, a rope ladder, climbing rope, or a swing. While a treehouse blends best into the tree if it is built from hardwood, you could paint it a bright color and turn it into the central focus of the yard.

When planning child-friendly outdoor space, divide the available space into specific activity areas, using a scale plan if necessary. Ideally, there should be a running-around area, a deck designated for a table and chairs, and a secret play area, perhaps with a sandbox, usually at one end

By incorporating a few imaginative features into your yard, you will fire your children's imagination. A densely planted area, with a mirror on one wall, becomes a fairy grotto at the bottom of the garden, while a *trompe-l'oeil* gate suggests a secret world beyond. Break up a boring expanse of lawn with pretty picket fencing or fast-growing plants like bamboo, so there are secret spots for a private picnic or games of hide-and-seek. If possible, secure any exits from the garden, so that everyone is safe. Provide children with fun equipment so playing outdoors becomes an extension of inside. Here, Yasmin and Sarah let off steam with a giant ball.

of the yard. If you have older boys, you might instead want to allocate the end of the yard for football. Keep their scuffed piece of lawn out of sight by disguising it with a dividing section of wall or fence. In a bold modern yard, the wall could be turned into an architectural feature and painted a vibrant hue. Alternatively, integrate it into the rest of the garden by growing a flowering climber over it, and put in a pretty wall-mounted fountain. Think about imaginative ways to mark out the different activity areas. You could use tall plants, stepping stones set into the lawn, or trellis. And, although vast, manicured lawns are great for running around, and an ideal spot for the trampoline or climbing gym, kids do appreciate a touch of nature's chaos. Section off a part of the yard,

" Friends come over and the children can do their thing—having a pool is the greatest form of entertainment. "

DEB, MOTHER

plant it with bamboo, palms, wild grasses, and flowers, and you won't see your kids for dust.

If your outdoor plot is very small, such divisions are impossible, so concentrate instead on making the space attractive for grown-ups, yet user-friendly for kids. Laying the same flooring throughout instantly unifies a tiny yard: limestone, wooden decking, quarry tiles, and cement are all good options. Don't sacrifice running-around space by having large flowerbeds: stick to robust, evergreen shrubs in tubs, which not only look stylish but will also withstand the odd knock from a football. Hard surfaces are practical, but children also appreciate a spot of grass where they can flop down and read. A circle of lawn, however small, can look very chic surrounded by limestone flagstones, and allows space to pitch a tiny tent.

Provide access to sand and water in the yard, and you'll keep younger children amused for hours. Readymade sandboxes often come in garish colors, so consider building your own. If you are creating a small yard from scratch, a sandbox can be inset into the paving, but it's essential to fit a tight cover so the sand is protected at night. An outdoor faucet, easy enough for a child to turn on, means little ones can fill buckets or water the plants to their hearts' content. It's relatively easy to put in a hot-water faucet, too. Add a giant planter beneath it, and the children can indulge in a marvelous hot bath in the open air. With safety in mind, a fish pond is best saved until the teenage years. But it's still possible to enjoy water features: choose a wall-mounted fountain with self-circulating pump, so the water goes round and round, instead of pooling into a potentially fatal trough.

PREVIOUS PAGE: **A great child-friendly backyard has a structure to climb on, a quiet area for drawing or eating, and a stretch of grass to run around on. Relaxed planting means kids don't have to steer clear of special flowers; or teach them to respect the garden by giving them their own patch. If there's no natural shade, provide a sun umbrella or little tent, or grow a creeper over an arch.** THIS PAGE AND OPPOSITE: **Well supervised, kids will spend hours playing in water. Provide inflatable boats and animals, plus flippers and snorkels, and blow-up rings for younger ones. For Bo, Tucker, Gibson, and Gussie, the pool is the place to be.**

THIS PAGE AND OPPOSITE:
Instead of fretting about the
limitations of a small, urban
outdoor space, concentrate
instead on finding fun ways
to equip it for play. With a
water pipe, wading pool,
and hose, this small rooftop
eyrie is an irresistible draw
for three-year-old Teresa on
a hot day. Water play
equipment is inexpensive
and fun: look for giant water
pistols, or spray and jet
attachments for a
conventional garden
sprinkler. Pick a rigid rather
than blow-up style of
wading pool, as it can
double as a sandbox.

Eating outdoors is exciting for children and fun for adults, too. Choose all-weather metal or wooden furniture that can be left out year round, so that impromptu alfresco meals are easy. Look for miniature versions of teak garden furniture or tiny deckchairs in bright canvas. Building a wooden arbor for trailing flowering plants or a vine provides essential shade. And a family barbecue, beneath its leafy cover, is the stuff childhood memories are made of.

source list

FURNITURE

Casa Kids
106 Ferris Street
Brooklyn, NY 11231
(718) 694-0272
www.casakids.com
Imaginative designs by architect
Roberto Gil. Ingenious chairs,
storage and a raised bed, in
funky colors.

Ethan Allen Kids
Visit www.ethanallen.com or call
1-888-EAHELP1 for details of
your nearest store.
www.ethanallen.com
Large selection of every type of
children's furniture, as well as
decorative accessories.

For Mercy's Sake
3911 Kandy Drive
Austin, TX 78749
(512) 665 0882
www.formercysake.com
Handpainted children's furniture.

Fun Time Designs Inc.
#375–2600 Granville Street
Vancouver, B.C. Canada
V6H 3V3
(800) 977-3443
Furniture featuring kids' favorite
cartoon characters.

Homevisions
Visit www.homevisions.com or call
(800) 651 1415 for a catalog.
Fun and funky furniture, cute
accessories, outdoor gym sets,
and playcenters.

Little Colorado
4450 Lipan Street
Denver, CO 80211
(303) 964-3212
www.littlecolorado.com
Quality handcrafted children's
furniture and gorgeous toys,
including a kid's kitchen center.

MB Furniture
2311 Avenue U
Brooklyn, NY 11229
(718) 332-1500
www.mbfurniture.com
Shop online for cribs, bassinets,
and highchairs.

My Second Step
116 Harold Avenue
Swansboro, NC 28584
(910) 326 6939
Handpainted, personalized
children's step stools.

Pottery Barn
Visit www.potterybarn.com or call
(800) 993 4923 for details of
your nearest store.
One-stop shop for babies and
kids' rooms. Furniture, beddings,
rugs, window coverings, storage,
toys, and accessories.

Tuffyland
H. Wilson Company
555 West Taft Drive
South Holland, IL 60473
(800) 245-7224
www.tuffyland.com
Sturdy, colorful children's activity
tables and chairs, plus storage
and computer workstations.

Wildzoo Furniture
63025 O. B. Riley Road #9
Bend, OR 97701
(888) 543-8588
www.wildzoo.com
Well-designed wooden computer
desks and play tables.

STORAGE

Frick and Frack's Toy Storage
1470 Route 23 North
Wayne, NJ 07470
(973) 696-6701
www.frickandfrack.com
Handpainted toy benches,
rocking chairs, and trunks.

Hold Everything
P.O. Box 7807
San Francisco, CA 94120
(800) 840-3596
www.holdeverything.com
Everything for storage.

IKEA
Call (800) 254-IKEA or visit
www.ikea.com for the location of
your nearest store.
Kids' furniture and accessories.

BEDS

Blackwelders
Visit www.homefurnish.com/
blackwelders or call (800) 438-
0201 for a retailer near you.
Kids' beds in a large range of
styles, from New England-style
bunk beds to Plantation-style
sleigh beds. Matching bedroom
furniture also available.

buybuyBABY
1683 Rockville Pike
Rockville, MD 20852
(301) 984-1122
www.buybuybaby.com
Cribs, cradles, and bassinets, as
well as safety equipment.

The Land of Nod
900 W. North Avenue
Chicago, IL 60622
(312) 475 9903
Visit www.landofnod.com or call
(800) 933 9904 for a catalog.
Tasteful beds, furniture and
dozens of other irresistable items
for babies' and kids' rooms.

BED LINEN

Babies "R" Us
Visit www.babiesrus.com or call
(800) BABY RUS for a retailer
near you.
Complete line of linens for
babies.

Garnet Hill
Visit www.garnethill.com or call
(800) 870 3513 for a catalog.
Colorful, high-quality children's
bedlinen and some kid's clothes
in the finest natural fibers. Visit
the website for details of their
outlet stores.

Night and Day
7033 E 1st Avenue
Scottsdale, AZ 85251
(480) 481-5106
Babies' and children's linens,
decorative pillows, and robes.

Wamsutta

Springs Industries Inc.
P.O. Box 70
Fort Mill, SC 29716
(800) 831-1488
www.wamsutta.com
Baby bedding and character-themed bedlinen for toddlers and older kids.

Westpoint Stevens

Visit www.westpointstevens.com or call (800) 533-8229 for a retailer near you.
Bedding for kids and teens, including Disney character bed linen and baby crib sets.

FABRICS

Calico Corners

Call (800) 213-6366 or visit www.calicocorners.com for a retailer near you.
Wide range of fabric.

Kravet Fabrics Inc.

225 Central Avenue S.
Bethpage, NY 11714
(800) 648-5728
www.kravet.com
Variety of textures including chenille, woven, and multi-purpose fabrics.

Waverly

Call (800) 432-5881 or visit www.decoratewaverly.com for a retailer near you.
Fabrics, wallpaper, carpets, blinds, accessories, and baby furnishings.

PAINTS

Crayola Paints

Call (800) 344-0400 or visit www.benjaminmoore.com for a retailer near you.
Washable latex paint, including glitter, glow in the dark, and chalkboard varieties.

The Old Fashioned Milk Paint Co., Inc.

436 Main Street
P.O. Box 222
Groton, MA 01450
(978) 448-6336
www.milkpaint.com
Non-fade colors made to a traditional milk paint recipe.

WallNutz

Visit www.wallnutz.com or call (877) 360-3325 for details of your nearest retailer.
Attractive, inexpensive, paint-by-number wall mural kits for decorating kids' rooms.

BATHROOMS

Bed, Bath & Beyond

620 6th Avenue
New York, NY 10011
(800) GO BEYOND
www.bedbathandbeyond.com
Modern bathroom accessories.

The Bumblebee Bush

Bowling Green Kentucky
(270) 393-BEES
www.bumblebeebush.com
Bath and linens for babies.

Smart-Babies.com

P.O. Box 530374
Henderson, NV 89053-0374
(877) 310-6647
www.smart-babies.com
Bath toys.

ACCESSORIES

babystyle.com

Visit www.babystyle.com or call (877) 378 9537 for a catalog.
Nursery furniture, bedding and accessories.

Bell Sports, Inc.

Call (800) 456-BELL or visit www.bellbikehelmets.com for a retailer near you.
Bike helmets.

ChildSecure

10660 Pine Haven
N. Bethesda, MD 20852
(800) 450-6530
Safety guidance and childproofing.

City Cricket

215 W 10th St
New York, NY 10014
(212) 242-2258
www.citycricket.com
Blankets, vintage-style toys, and flatware for babies and kids.

Claire's Stores Inc.

Visit www.claires.com or call (800) CLAIRES for your nearest store.
Mall-based retailer of well-priced pre-teen accessories.

dELiAs

Natick Mall
1245 Worcester Street,
Suite 2416
Natick, MA 01760
(508) 647-9357
www.delias.com
Funky girls' bedding and unusual accessories.

Kid Carpet

Visit www.kidcarpet.com or call (888) 308-4884.
High-quality carpet and rugs for playrooms and kids' rooms.

Swings N' Things

23052 Lake Forest Drive
Laguna Hills, CA 92653
(949) 770-7799
www.swingsnthingsca.com
Manufacturer of premium quality residential playground equipment.

Urban Outfitters

3111 Main Street N.W.
Washington, D.C.
(202) 342-1012
www.urbanoutfitters.com
Kitsch accessories, including funky shower curtains and sparkly lamps.

picture credits

All photographs by Debi Treloar unless otherwise stated.

Key: l left r right b below t top c center

2 An apartment in London by Malin Iovino Design; 3 Vincent & Frieda Plasschaert's house in Brugge, Belgium; 5 The Boyes' home in London designed by Circus Architects; 12–13 Victoria Andreae's house in London; 14–15 Ab Rogers & Sophie Braimbridge's House, London, designed by Richard Rogers for his mother. Furniture design by KRD–Kitchen Rogers Design; 16–17 Sophie Eadie's house in London; 18–19 Rudi, Melissa & Archie Thackry's house in London; 20 c & l An apartment in London by Malin Iovino Design; 20 r Designed by Sage and Coombe Architects, New York; 21 Vincent & Frieda Plasschaert's house in Brugge, Belgium; 24–25 Julia & David O'Driscoll's house in London; 26–27 Ben Johns & Deb Waterman Johns' house in Georgetown; 28–29 Michele Johnson's house in London designed by Nico Rensch Architeam; 30–31 The Zwirner's loft in New York; 34–35 Designed by Sage and Coombe Architects, New York; 36–37 The Boyes' home in London designed by Circus Architects; 38 Designed by Sage and Coombe Architects, New York; 42–47 Victoria Andreae's house in London; 48 Sera Hersham-Loftus' house in London; 50 l Suzanne & Christopher Sharp's house in London; 50 r–51 The Zwirner's loft in New York; 53–55 Sudi Pigott's house in London; 56 Elizabeth Alford & Michael Young's loft in New York; 57 Sophie Eadie's house in London; 58–59 Julia & David O'Driscoll's house in London; 62–65 Eben & Nica Cooper's bedroom, the Cooper family playroom; 67 Sue & Lars-Christian Brask's house in London designed by Susie Atkinson Design; 68–69 Pear Tree Cottage, Somerset, mural by Bruce Munro; 70–71 Suzanne & Christopher Sharp's house in London; 72 An apartment in New York designed by Steven Learner Studio; 73 Vincent & Frieda Plasschaert's house in Brugge, Belgium; 74–75 Ben Johns & Deb Waterman Johns' house in Georgetown; 78–79 Vincent & Frieda Plasschaert's house in Brugge, Belgium; 80 bl Sophie Eadie's house in London; 80 bc David & Macarena Wheldon's house in London designed by Fiona McLean; 80 br Sera Hersham-Loftus' house in London; 81 bl & br Ben Johns & Deb Waterman Johns' house in Georgetown; 84 l Ab Rogers & Sophie Braimbridge's House, London, designed by Richard Rogers for his mother. Furniture design by KRD–Kitchen Rogers Design; 84 br Designed by Ash Sakula Architects; 85 An apartment in New York designed by Steven Learner Studio; 86 Sudi Pigott's house in London; 87 Ben Johns & Deb Waterman Johns' house in Georgetown; 88–89 photographer Caroline Arber/Archie & Pink, London E1, loft designed by Will White; 90–91 David & Macarena Wheldon's house in London designed by Fiona McLean; 92–93 Vincent & Frieda Plasschaert's house in Brugge, Belgium; 94 tl Designed by Ash Sakula Architects; 94 b An apartment in London by Malin Iovino Design; 95 Ben Johns & Deb Waterman Johns' house in Georgetown; 96 main An apartment in London by Malin Iovino Design; 96 tcr, lc & lb Belén Moneo & Jeff Brock's apartment in New York designed by Moneo Brock Studio; 96 tr Ben Johns & Deb Waterman Johns' house in Georgetown; 97 main Elizabeth Alford & Michael Young's loft in New York; 97 tl & tr An apartment in London by Malin Iovino Design; 98–99 Hans & Lena Blomberg's house designed by Orefelt Associates; 100 tl An apartment in London by Malin Iovino Design; 100 tr Vincent & Frieda Plasschaert's house in Brugge, Belgium; 100 bl An apartment in New York designed by Steven Learner Studio; 100 bc Eben & Nica Cooper's bedroom, the Cooper family playroom, 100 br Ab Rogers & Sophie Draimbridge's House, London, designed by Richard Rogers for his mother. Furniture design by KRD–Kitchen Rogers Design; 102–103 The Zwirner's loft in New York; 106–107 Designed by Ash Sakula Architects; 108 l Victoria Andreae's house in London; 108 r Sophie Eadie's house in London; 109 l David & Macarena Wheldon's house in London designed by Fiona McLean; 109 r The Zwirner's loft in New York; 112 l Victoria Andreae's house in London; 112 r The Zwirner's loft in New York; 113 l & r Designed by Sage and Coombe Architects, New York; 116 & 117 b Belén Moneo & Jeff Brock's apartment in New York designed by Moneo Brock Studio; 117 t & c Designed by Ash Sakula; 120 David & Macarena Wheldon's house in London designed by Fiona McLean ; 121 Designed by Sage and Coombe Architects, New York; 122 t & 123 Victoria Andreae's house in London; 126–127 Michele Johnson's house in London designed by Nico Rensch Architeam; 128 Victoria Andreae's house in London; 129 t Charlotte Crosland's house in London; 129 b Ben Johns & Deb Waterman Johns' house in Georgetown; 130–131 playhouse by Dan Levy; 133 main & tc, cr, & br Sarah Gredley's house in London, tree house designed by Kim Woolfe-Murray; 134–135 Ben Johns & Deb Waterman Johns' house in Georgetown.

architects & designers

Elizabeth Alford Design
60 Thomas Street
New York, NY 10013
USA
t. 212 385 2185
f. 212 385 2186
e. esa799@banet.net
56; 97 main

Ash Sakula Architects
24 Rosebery Avenue
London EC1R 4SX
t. 00 44 20 7837 9735
www.ashsak.com
84 br; 94 tl; 106–107;
117 t & c

Circus Architects
1a Summer's Street
London EC1R 5BD
t. 00 44 20 7833 1999
f. 00 44 20 7833 1888
5; 36–37

Charlotte Crosland
Wingrave Crosland Interiors
t. 00 44 20 8960 9442
f. 00 44 20 8960 9714
129 t

Malin Iovino Design
t. 00 44 20 7252 3542
f. 00 44 20 7252 3542
e. iovino@btconnect.com
2; 20 c & l; 94 b; 96 main;
97 tl & tr; 100 tl

**KRD–Kitchen Rogers
Design**
t. 00 44 20 8944 7088
e. ab@krd.demon.co.uk
14–15; 84 l; 100 br

Dan Levy
artist / woodworker
34 Summerfield Avenue
London NW6 6JY
t. 00 44 20 8969 8428
130–131

Fiona McLean
McLean Quinlan Architects
t. 00 44 20 8767 1633
80 bc; 90–91; 109 l; 120

**Jeff Brock and Belén
Moneo**
Moneo Brock Studio
371 Broadway, 2nd floor
New York, NY 10013
USA
www.moneobrock.com
96 tcr, lc & lb; 116 & 117
tr

Bruce Munro
Mural commissions
t. 00 44 1749 813 898
f. 00 44 1749 813 515
e. brucemunro@freenet.co.uk
68–69

Nico Rensch Architeam
t. 00 44 1424 445885
www.architeam.co.uk
28–29; 126–127

Orefelt Associates
43 Pall Mall Deposit
124–128 Barlby Road
London W10 6BL
t. 00 44 20 8960 2560
98–99

**Sage and Coombe
Architects**
205 Hudson Street
Suite 1002
New York, NY 10013
USA
t. 212 226 9600
f. 212 226 8456
www.sageandcoombe.com
20 r; 34–35; 38; 113 l
& r; 121

Susie Atkinson Design
t. 07768 814 134
67

Steven Learner Studio
307 Seventh Avenue
New York, NY 10001
USA
t. 212 741 8583
f. 212 741 2180
www.stevenlearnerstudio.com
72; 85; 100 bl

Kim Woolfe-Murray
Urban & Country Tree
Houses
34 North Junction Road
Edinburgh EH6 6HP
t. 00 44 131 553 5554
133 main, tc, cr & br

Will White Design
326 Portobello Road
London W10 5RU
t. 00 44 20 8964 8052
f. 00 44 20 8964 8050
e. willwhite.design@virgin.net
88–89

index